A Sunset Pictorial

GHOST TOWNS of the WEST

Sunset
GHOST TOWNS

Text and Photographs by William Carter

LANE MAGAZINE & BOOK COMPANY

of the WEST

Supervising Editor: Jack McDowell

Design Consultants: Fetzer-Conover Graphics
Layout: Henry Rasmussen
Cartography & Illustrations: Basil C. Wood

MENLO PARK, CALIFORNIA

CONTENTS

"THE CASTLE," VIRGINIA CITY, NEVADA

METHODIST CHURCH, BODIE, CALIFORNIA

SILVER MILL, ELKHORN, MONTANA

RESIDENCE, GILMORE, IDAHO

HOUSE, NEAR MOGOLLON, NEW MEXICO

ACKNOWLEDGEMENTS

Title Page: Bodie, California.

All photographs, except those listed below, are by William Carter.

Arizona Pioneers Historical Museum: 216, 217 (bottom left, bottom right), 219, 222 (bottom), 223 (top left and right), 236 (bottom right, top), 237 (all), 239, 243 (top). Bancroft Library: 27, 34 (top), 36 (top left, center left, bottom right), 74 (right), 162, 203 (bottom right), 204 (top), 205 (right). Dorothy Benrimo: 250 (top left, top center), 251 (top right). Barbara Braasch: 61 (top right). British Columbia Provincial Archives: 196 (top), 204 (bottom). Richard Weymouth Brooks: 58 (bottom). Don Bufkin: 240 (original map). California Division of Mines and Geology: 41 (top). California Highway Department: 26 (bottom). California Historical Society: 26 (top), 40. California State Library: 16, 20, 21 (top), 30, 35 (bottom), 36 (top right), 76 (left). Centennial Museum, Vancouver: 203 (top left). Glenn Christiansen: 38. John N. DeHaas, Jr.: 136 (bottom). Denver Public Library Western Collection: 108, 112 (bottom, top right), 113 (right), 123 (bottom), 144, 151 (top right), 152 (bottom), 154 (top left, top right, bottom), 155 (right), 178. Richard Dillon Collection: 74 (left). Lewis Douglas Collection: 222 (center), 249 (top). Carlos Elmer: 106 (top). Lambert Florin: 152 (top), 161 (center right), 206 (center left). Gerald R. Fredrick: 49 (bottom). Cecil Helms: 49 (top). Walter Houk: 56 (top), 61 (bottom left). Huntington Library: 21 (bottom). Bob Iacopi: 60 (bottom right). Idaho Historical Society: 112 (top left), 118 (bottom), 122 (bottom right), 174, 182 (top). Karl Kernberger: 9 (bottom), 213 (top left), 215, 224, 242, 250 (bottom left), 252 (bottom left). Ralph Looney Collection: 223 (center), 228, 230 (top and center), 231, 250 (bottom right). Los Angeles County Museum of Natural History: 24 (top), 100 (top). Gar Lunney: 206 (bottom right). Mackay School of Mines: 71, 78 (bottom), 94 (top).

Ells Marugg: 19 (bottom), 39 (center right). Metropolitan Museum of Art: 37. Montana Historical Society: 118 (top left, top right), 122 (left), 124 (bottom), 145 (right), 157, 249 (bottom). Nell Murbarger Collection: 58 (top), 59 (bottom), 97 (top), 253 (top left). Museum of New Mexico: 155 (left), 208, 213 (top right), 217 (top left, top right), 225 (bottom), 236 (bottom left). Tom Myers: 19 (top), 46, 52, 53 (top), 60 (top center). National Archives: 17 (top). National Park Service: 146 (top and bottom), 147 (top). Nevada Historical Society: 62, 72, 76, 82, 86, 87 (top and bottom), 95 (top and bottom), 98 (left). Nevada State Museum: 79. Don Normark: 171 (bottom). Rodman Paul: 41 (original data for curve, courtesy University of Nebraska Press). Silver Nugget Museum, Tombstone, Arizona: 241. Larry Smith: 48 (top). Society of California Pioneers: 17 (bottom). Sutro Library: 24 (bottom). Texas Highway Department: 253 (bottom left). Mike Tilden: 48 (bottom). University of Oregon Special Collections: 182 (bottom), 202 (top right, bottom). Utah State Historical Society: 114 (top and bottom), 123 (top), 158. Darrow M. Watt: 39 (bottom right). Todd Webb: 66, 250 (top right). Robert Weinstein Collection: 12. Western Ways Features: 144 (bottom left), 168, 169 (top and bottom). Edward Weston: 85. S. C. Wilson: 171 (top). Don Wright: 117 (top).

Page 205: Quotation from Greever, William S. *The Bonanza West.* Norman, Oklahoma. University of Oklahoma Press. pp. 341-2. Page 214: Quotation from Jenkinson, Michael. *Ghost Towns of New Mexico.* Albuquerque, New Mexico. The University of New Mexico Press, 1967. p. 32.

Our Ghost Towns Will Not Be Here Much Longer

Until recently, no one thought twice about the defunct towns scattered across the West. The past was too recent, and we were all too preoccupied with progress. Nobody cared if old walls and artifacts disappeared, and—by a more or less natural process of attrition—they did.

Suddenly the situation has changed. Old artifacts have soared in value. The rollicking, individualistic spirit of the frontier has come to seem an antidote to urban greyness. Everyone is taking to the back-roads, looking for destinations—and the frail ghost towns are an obvious target. So critical has the situation become that, if present trends continue, *many of our ghost towns are in danger of disappearing altogether.*

They deserve a better fate, constituting as they do some of the few visible reminders of the West's brief past. How can they be saved? The answer is not a simple one, because the threats are as varied as the towns themselves.

Year by year, nature still takes its toll. Every winter, heavy snows collapse another roof or two. When the roof goes, the walls are often quick to follow. A flood wrecks the frame buildings of Sandon, British Columbia; a desert twister carries away adobe walls in Shakespeare, New Mexico. Timbers rot; pack rats scamper through scanty floorings. Slowly, the weeds and earth reclaim their own.

But the man-made dangers are far worse. Whether set carelessly or deliberately, fire can quickly wipe out a block of hundred-year-old false fronts. As urban population pressures drive people farther and farther afield, a ghost in a beautiful setting—such as Crested Butte, Colorado—becomes a natural target for vacation home-building. Tourist-conscious commercialization rears its head in one locale after the next. Prompted by tax laws and other factors, mining companies and other owners raze old structures: today, wonderful Tyrone, New Mexico, is gone. As old brick becomes valuable, once-classic Aurora, Nevada, becomes a ghost of a ghost. Bombing ranges eclipse Fairview and other central Nevada mining camps; and some of the pilots try out their machine guns on the tall smokestacks of Belmont, where people still live.

More wanton yet are the isolated acts of thieves and vandals. The frequency of such destruction has risen sharply since the mid-1960's, and this is the main threat to the continued existence of the true ghost towns. One factor has undoubtedly been the upsurge in Western back-road travel. Snowmobiles, for instance, afford access to a mountain ghost like Garnet, Montana, during a season when no one can stay to protect it. As a result, the Garnet Hotel lost its fine stair railing and newel post in the winter of 1969-70, and someone burned down the grocery store in 1970-71.

What, then, can be done? One can appeal to people to respect property and the past—to think twice before taking away what others might enjoy.

What else? The solutions depend on local conditions. Although transforming a ghost town into a museum can kill its mood, we do have examples of sensitive official action. At the State Park of Bodie, California, for instance, a concept of "arrested decay" struck a sensible balance between too much preservation and too little, the restraining hand remaining largely unseen.

Where whole towns are individually owned, the situation varies widely. Ruby, Arizona, is effectively sealed off to tourists. Helena, California, and St. Elmo, Colorado, welcome visitors under the owners' watchful eye. Other privately owned ghosts rely on such signs as "Survivors Will be Prosecuted"—with varying results.

Here and there, dedicated persons or groups—from elderly ladies to idealistic college students—have taken on the task of benevolently watching over some town or structure. Commercial development itself, though not necessarily bad, depends on the character of the town in the first place, and on the taste and tractibility of the developers.

There is no one solution. But on every level, we'll do well to realize that our past belongs to us all—and to none of us alone.

THE WESTERN GHOST TOWN

EXCITEMENT ...THEN A STEEP DECLINE

COURTHOUSE, VIRGINIA CITY, NEVADA

We're a young, restless people. America's momentum toward an ever-new frontier profoundly affected our outlook, our habits, our communities. Among the most visible signs of this restlessness are the hundreds of ghost towns strewn across the western states. As one authority pointed out, deserted communities are nothing new in the world, but only the American West propagated them in wholesale quantities.

How were these towns born, and why did they die? Most were mining towns. Of the many factors which prompted Americans to head west in the 1800's, none held such glittering promise as the continuing news of gold and silver strikes. Prior to the California gold rush of 1848, the westward movement was a relatively gradual affair: patient explorers, trappers, and missionaries were followed by farmers, herdsmen, and small tradesmen. But gold was an explosive fuse, sparking a dramatic growth of population and shattering the trends of earlier settlement. The miner's eye, agleam with the

STORE, VIRGINIA CITY, NEVADA

RESIDENCE, HILLSBOROUGH, NEW MEXICO

prospect of quick cash, also gleamed with thoughts of the goods and services his "poke" could buy. Totally different in character from the slow-going farmer, who came west to be self-sufficient, the restless Forty-niner and his successors demanded saloons and hotels, banks and stagecoaches, noise and excitement. In answer to his needs, rowdy boomtowns blossomed, creating what has been aptly termed an urban frontier.

Yet these instant towns soon proved anew that "mining is a good way to pioneer a territory, but a poor way to hold it." The boomers' roots went only as deep as the high-grade ore. When that began to give out, they were always ready to run off after some new bonanza, sending the mining camp into a steep decline that often turned it into a ghost. Only mining could create such high-priced towns in the wilderness —and only mining could deplete their economic base so quickly. The footloose character of the prospectors, and the seeming endlessness of the virgin frontier, reinforced the up-and-down process repeated hundreds of times across the early West.

Also running counter to the earlier trends of pioneer settlement was the tendency of the mining frontier to move from west to east during its prime phases. When California's placer deposits dwindled in the 1850's, a new bonanza east of the Sierra, in Nevada's Comstock, lured hordes of "Old Californians," as they were called, into the little-known Great Basin area. Then gold was discovered in Colorado, and the Pike's Peak rush was on. From Colorado the miners fanned out into the other Rocky Mountain territories. (The Northwest lacked any clear trend, and the Southwest was last to be developed because of special problems.)

As the nineteenth century progressed, many of the early mining areas, having all but died, got a second lease on life as a result of advancing technology and transportation. While the early miners took out what they could by simple methods, the advent of the railroad, growing financial sophistication, and the industrial revolution made profitable the extraction of more refractory, hard-rock ores. In this phase, many old towns were revitalized and many new ones born. Yet these, too, dwindled in time; and many of today's best-preserved ghost towns and mining camps derive from this second stage of the mining frontier, which stretched well into the twentieth century.

Americans have not stopped being restless, and ghost towns have not stopped being made. It is true that today's miner often lives in a trailer camp or large town and drives to work, and that while company towns are still built in certain remote areas, they are seldom merely abandoned when the job is done. Yet at least one good-sized copper town—Bisbee, Arizona—now appears headed toward ghost-town status. By 1971, population had declined from 25,000 to 8,000 as one huge mine after the next was being closed.

Large-scale population movements are still going on, too. Between 1960 and 1971, Nevada's population mushroomed by 71%, Arizona's by 36%. At the same time, hundreds of small agricultural towns in the Great Plains were dying. In Sheridan County, North Dakota, which lost 26% of its population during the 1960's, Lincoln Valley became a total ghost town, with others not far behind; there were towns with similar stories all the way south to the Mexican border. Yet the scenic Rocky Mountain States, adjoining the plains States on the west, were enjoying a rural land boom. And in an era when Federal legislation was priming the development of new communities throughout America, the construction of some was halted by court order because of pollution problems—creating, in effect, ecological ghost towns. The dizzy rate of these changes would seem astonishing to any people other than Westerners.

Though still young and restless, we Westerners have begun to feel a need for roots—for a sense of the past. One indication is a deepening interest in old buildings and artifacts. Suddenly, ghost towns nobody wanted have come to seem a valuable heritage, priceless remnants of the rollicking frontier. Nowadays, ghost towns come in a variety of packages, suited for almost any temperament. There are the highly restored and commercialized versions such as Columbia, California, or Tombstone, Arizona; there are the dustblown, "pure" ghosts like Bodie, California, or Garnet, Montana; and there are many shades in between.

Just what constitutes a ghost town is inevitably a subjec-

COMMERCIAL BUILDING, VIRGINIA CITY, NEVADA

METHODIST CHURCH, VIRGINIA CITY, NEVADA

SALOON AND RESTAURANT, SHAKESPEARE, NEW MEXICO

tive question. A few purists argue that the place must have a population of zero. But so rigorous a definition would exclude many depopulated towns of interest to the average person. One authority proposes a looser concept, saying that a ghost town must simply be "a shadow of its former self"—as good a working concept as we've found. We have avoided those towns of which nothing, or almost nothing, remains; and we have stressed those in which there was a high proportion of unoccupied buildings of distinctive character. We've been as accurate as possible as of 1971. But, as has been pointed out, the western landscape is changing rapidly, and no one can say what may happen to any of these quaint communities in years to come. The reader is strongly advised to use his own judgment in visiting any ghost town, and to make local inquiries as to safety, property ownership, and trespass laws.

How fortunate that photography was invented less than twenty years before James Marshall discovered gold in California! The photographer's art grew up alongside the mining frontier, and our most vivid impressions of those zany times are preserved in the silvered images housed in precious collections throughout the West. Ghost towns are also good targets for modern shutterbugs. In addition to the normal lens, a wide-angle lens—such as a 28mm lens on a 35mm camera —is quite useful in ghost town shooting; and don't overlook the uses of macro lenses and other close-up devices. For color under wide-open skies and at higher elevations, use a skylight or UV filter to correct excessive bluishness. Dawn and dusk offer particularly expressive possibilities in all outdoor photography.

Finally, whether you go out into the field or stay in an armchair, we hope you'll find the same thing a young Montana diarist found in 1864: that "truth and the marvelous go hand in hand when Young America finds a good gold gulch."

SEEKING THEIR FORTUNES in the newly-discovered gold fields, a motley throng of restless adventurers poured into California. They built wild mining camps which quickly became ghost towns when the gold ran out.

1

CALIFORNIA
EXPLODES!
1848...

A JANUARY MORNING, CRISP AND CLEAR. The sawmill foreman was up early. He was a loner—moody, and hard to get along with. But he was a good builder, anxious to complete the new structure. While his men dallied over breakfast, he was already busy down at the river. Each day the men cut the mill race ditch deeper, and each night the foreman let the river rush through it to sweep away the debris. Soon the current would be strong enough to power saws. James Marshall closed the sluice gate and waded down the drained, muddy ditch, checking its depth. Then something caught his eye. Stooping, he reached into the shallow water. What he found changed the course of American history.

"Boys," he later told the men, "I believe I have found a gold mine."

"Gold!" shouted storekeeper Sam Brannan, galloping through the streets of San Francisco, waving his hat. "Gold from the American River!" Traces of gold had been found before in California, but had caused no stir. Now, in 1848, it was suddenly different. As one San Francisco newspaper lamented, "The field is left half planted, the house half built, and everything neglected but the manufacture of shovels and pickaxes." By fall, when the news reached eastern America, the whole country went wild. Gold-seeking "Argonauts" from all over the world poured into California, multiplying its population sixteen-fold in four years, and doubling the world's gold output.

CALIFORNIA AND ITS GHOST TOWNS

Incredible camps and towns sprang up, with names such as You Bet, Lousy Ravine, Volcano, Bogus Thunder, and Git-Up-And-Git. Like the footloose men who founded them, the towns lived fast and often died young. Many were abandoned as suddenly as they had appeared. Others, jerry-built of canvas, wood, and whatever else lay handy, were devastated by raging fires, only to be reconstructed before the embers cooled. In a short time, the lawless frontier began to acquire more permanent buildings—brick and stone structures, often with iron doors and shutters that helped guard precious gold dust which had become the prime medium of exchange. But when, inevitably, the gold gave out, these more substantial towns, too, lost their populations and became ghosts which survive down to the present.

Most of California's ghost towns and semi-ghost towns are thus direct products of the gold rush. They lie in the regions known as the Mother Lode and Northern Mines, east of the Central Valley along the Sierra foothills. Because the area declined in importance but did not die completely, few of these historic settlements are "pure" ghosts; they remain, nonetheless, moody and charming remnants of the glory that once was.

Second in interest is an area farther north, around Mt. Shasta and Weaverville. Gold fever raged here at almost the same time as in the Mother Lode, and the style of many of the surviving buildings and artifacts is remarkably similar to that along Highway 49.

The California ghost towns lying east and southeast of the Sierra are the residue of mining rushes which occurred later in the century. Since these belong topographically to the Great Basin area, they are treated in Chapter Two.

Finally, around the turn of the century, the deserts of Southern California attracted sporadic little mining booms and busts, leaving some far-flung and very ghostly abandoned camps which hold much of the same somber fascination as the larger, more important ruins.

✗ True Ghost Town: Majority of buildings disused; few if any residents; no modern facilities.

⊛ Partial Ghost Town: Some disused buildings; some residents; limited facilities.

★ Tourist Ghost Town: Old structures refurbished to promote old-time atmosphere; modern facilities.

⁅40⁆ Interstate Highways

⁅80⁆ U.S. Highways

⁅95⁆ State Highways & Secondary Roads

NOTE: Map is as accurate as present information permits. Refer to detailed maps for minor roads, and always inquire locally about road conditions.

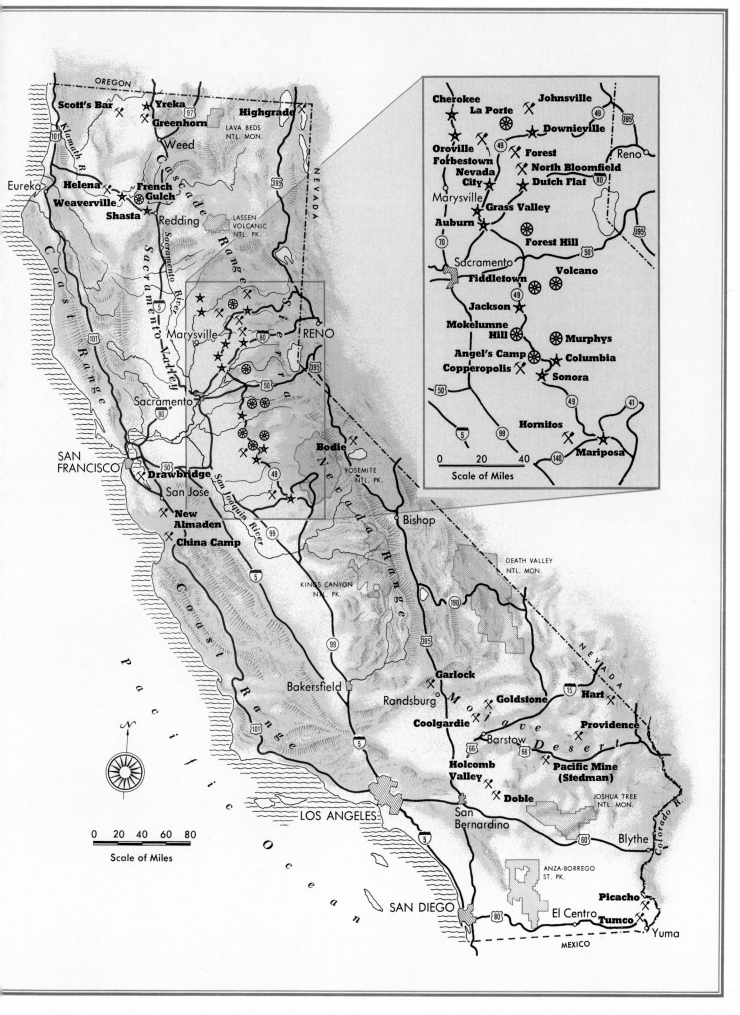

Marshall's Find: TRIGGERING THE BOOMTOWN BOOM

Someone would eventually have discovered California's gold; fate chose James Wilson Marshall, the eccentric foreman of John Sutter's sawmill at Coloma to first see the glint that would inflame a continent.

Marshall's immediate action—like much of his subsequent life—was not noticeably consistent. He put the first few nuggets into his slouch hat and showed them to his workers. They seemed unimpressed, although one of them, Bigler, noted in his diary, "This day some kind of mettle was found in the tail race that looks like goald, first discovered by James Martial, the Boss of the Mill."

Not until four days later did Marshall become obsessed with secrecy. On January 28, he rode wild-eyed and dripping wet into Sutter's fortress-like ranchero in the Central Valley and told his startled boss that he wanted to see him alone. "My God!" yelled the almost paranoiac Marshall, when an unsuspecting clerk wandered in with some papers. "Didn't I tell you to lock the door!" He and Sutter bolted the door and shoved a wardrobe in front of it. But the word was already out.

Though it took months for the news to spread, the subsequent gold rush dogged both Sutter and Marshall with misfortune. Sutter's workers abandoned their jobs in a thunderous quest for instant wealth in the hills, leaving thousands of dollars worth of wheat and hides to rot. His original dream of an agricultural empire ruined, Sutter tried to profit from the gold rush in a variety of ways, but never really succeeded. In the end, he moved to Pennsylvania and died, heartbroken, in 1880.

Marshall became a folk hero to others but a failure to himself. Stubbornly claiming supernatural powers, he wandered through the hills looking for more gold, but with little success. Other prospectors nevertheless assumed he had the Midas touch, and infuriated Marshall by following him and digging wherever he dug. More and more embittered, he came to believe that all the gold in California was rightfully his. Rejected by most camps, Marshall moved to Kelsey, now an obscure ghost town just east of Coloma, where he lived on odd jobs and handouts until his death in 1885.

SUPERNATURAL POWERS were attributed to James Marshall because his discovery ignited the California gold rush. But Marshall did not prosper. Long after the other miners had gone off after new bonanzas, he wandered sadly through the deserted hills, a ghost among ghost towns.

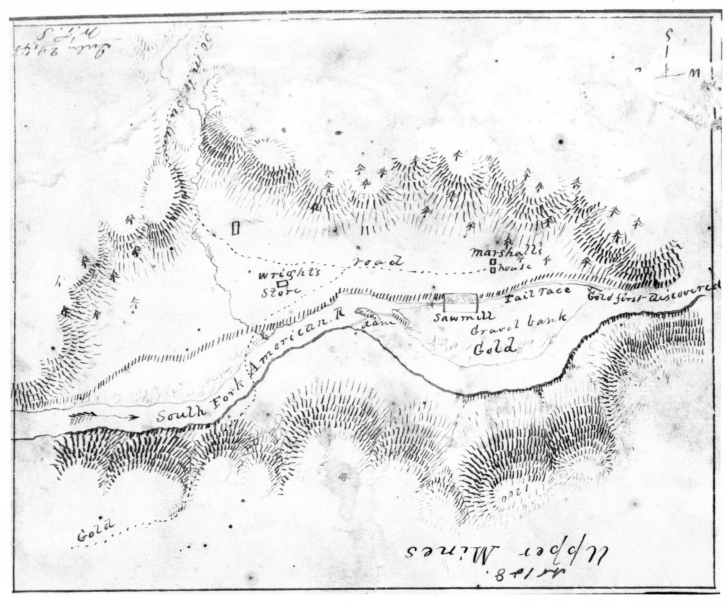

FAMOUS MAP, confirming California's gold discovery, was made in the summer of 1848 by William T. Sherman, then adjutant to California's military governor, later the famous Civil War general. Marshall's own map, probably made later, was childlike and fanciful.

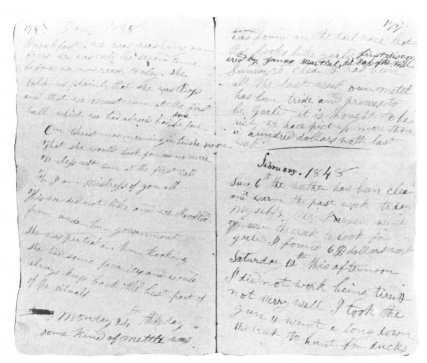

EXPERTS ARE CONVINCED of the truth of Marshall's story by the diary of Henry Bigler, a worker at Sutter's Mill. The entry of Jan. 24, 1848 reads: "This day some kind of mettle was found in the tail race that looks like goald, first discovered by James Martial, the Boss of the Mill."

COLOMA, CALIFORNIA
MOTHER OF MINING CAMPS

a GHOST TOWN worth seeing

From Auburn, on Interstate 80, head nineteen miles southeast on State 49. Coloma straddles the highway. Nearby towns of historical interest include Kelsey, Placerville, Georgetown, Volcanoville.

On the heels of James Marshall's find, Coloma sprang to bustling life. As the site of the earliest discovery, the town became a mecca and jumping-off point for the gold seekers who poured in from every corner of the globe. By 1849, thousands of residents milled through its narrow, sloping streets. Built in part with lumber cut at Sutter's Mill, scores of frame buildings went up, many of them wearing the false fronts which would soon typify mining camps throughout the West.

But of course the first strike was hardly the richest. The gold was soon gone from the picturesque little river canyon, and by 1851 Coloma was already moribund. Its population sank to two hundred by the 1870's. In contrast to the frantic early days, Coloma became, as one commentator observed, "a place of quiet serenity, of flower gardens and shaded lanes"—a character the community still possesses today.

There are a number of important things to see in this semi-ghost town which has been designated a State Park. The most apparent is Sutter's Mill, reconstructed in the original style of hand-hewn beams and mortise-and-tenon joints. Other worthwhile sights include Marshall's cabin, grave, and statue (on the hill near the two old churches); a number of authentic stone and brick buildings dating from the 1850's; and a shady park and museum, exhibiting pieces of old mining equipment.

POINTING toward the site of the discovery of gold in California, this statue of James Marshall stands on a hill near the cabin where he lived.

PAINSTAKINGLY RECONSTRUCTED
by the original hand methods, this exact
model of Sutter's Mill is a tourist highlight.
The river itself has changed its course
since the original discovery.

TRANQUILITY pervades the
once-rollicking gold camp.
The empty stone buildings
were occupied by Chinese,
who flocked to the gold
rush in great numbers.

JOINED YET DIVIDED by a sluice box bubbling with placer gold, stone-faced Caucasian miners pose with their equally sober Chinese counterparts. This daguerreotype is believed to have been made at the head of Auburn Ravine in 1852.

Polyglot Parade: THE MANY-HUED CAMPS

SIDE BY SIDE, white and black Argonauts shovel pay-dirt into a device known as a "long tom." A number of runaway slaves found their way to the California gold fields.

News of America's El Dorado reached Hawaii in June of 1848, Oregon in August, Mexico, Peru, and Chile by September. Almost immediately, boatloads of excited immigrants raced toward California. Americans from the eastern states did not arrive in any number before the middle of 1849. By then, an overland influx of Mexicans—or "Sonorans," as they were called in California—was well under way. Next came the Europeans, both from Europe itself and from England's penal colony in Australia. Last, but far from least, the Chinese appeared in the early 1850's.

Friction was immediate. The Mexicans and Latin Americans encountered so much hostility that they soon stopped coming entirely. The English, Scotch, Irish, and Welsh were accepted, and so were the Germans and Austrians; but the French were disliked because they kept to themselves, and became known as "Keskydees" because they kept asking "Qu'est-ce qu'il dit?" The native Indians were pushed aside.

The patient Chinese had the worst time of all. By 1852 some twenty thousand had settled in the gold area. Relegated to Chinatowns in the mining camps, and to the diggings nobody else wanted, they fought each other in Tong wars and served as the white man's scapegoat. *Hutchings' California Magazine* reported that a dispute among the Indians as to whether or not the Orientals were an inferior kind of Indian was settled by a Chinese being pushed into a raging river. When he drowned, it was agreed that Chinese were not Indians, because all Indians could swim.

Misunderstandings there were, and yet the ability of the new frontier to assimilate differences—and capitalize on the varied mining experience of the immigrants—was impressive. Witness this contemporary account: "The principal street of Coloma was alive with crowds of moving men, passing and repassing, laughing, talking, and all appearing in the best of humor: Negroes from the Southern States swaggering in the expansive feeling of runaway freedom; mulattoes from Jamaica trudging arm-in-arm with Kanakas from Hawaii; Peruvians and Chilians claiming affinity with the swarthier Mexicans: Frenchmen, Germans, and Italians fraternizing with one another and with the cockney fresh from the purlieus of St. Giles; an Irishman, with the dewdrop still in his eye, tracing relationship with the ragged Australian; Yankees from the Penobscot chatting and bargaining with the genial Oregonians; a few Celestials scattered here and there, their pigtails and conical hats recalling the strange pictures that took my boyish fancy while studying the geography of the East; last of all, a few Indians, the only indigenous creatures among all these exotics, lost, swallowed up. . . . It was a scene that no other country could ever immitate."

EXTREMELY RARE daguerreotype shows what appears to be American Indians working in the mines.

a GHOST TOWN worth seeing

From Stockton, take State 26 about thirty-four miles to State 12, four miles beyond Valley Springs, and turn right for four miles to San Andreas. Take State 49 eleven miles southeast to Altaville, turn left, go seven miles northeast to Murphys. Nearby spots of historical interest include Angels Camp, Sonora, Columbia, Copperopolis.

The bullet holes in the doorway are real, and so are the names in the register: Mark Twain, J. P. Morgan, Ulysses S. Grant, Black Bart. Today's visitor is invited to sign below. Upstairs, little plaques dedicate each room to some famous guest. Such touches of grandeur seem faintly incongruous, because the real charm of Murphys' Hotel is its air of amiable roughness. Heart of the matter is a fifty-foot, dark wood bar fronted by a heavy brass rail, on which the locals bang their feet loudly while sending their cackling laughter to ricochet off the dingy recesses of a lofty ceiling. Nobody has bothered to lock the front door since it first opened in 1856—somehow you don't need to be told.

Said to be the oldest continuously operated hotel in the United States, this iron-shuttered, flesh-colored gem is a good point of departure for exploring the rest of the venerable town. For, although Murphys is no pure ghost, the presence of its rough-hewn past is vivid.

Despite such tourist-conscious efforts as a well-stocked museum and an old bakery now converted to an antique shop, the town has avoided obvious commercialism. The single main street, heavily shaded with fine old locusts and elms, offers smooth-worn boardwalks, ancient benches, and a whole string of buildings dating from the 1850's—some vacant, but many still occupied. Murphys' rough splendors are crowned by two of the quaintest churches in the Mother Lode.

INDESTRUCTIBLE IRON shutters and safe of Murphys' Hotel date from the lawless 1850's, when such stout defenses were a virtual necessity in the Mother Lode. A tomb-like cement jail faces this wall of the Hotel.

PATINA OF THE PRESENT barely covers Murphys' many-layered past.
"Stephens Bro's. Cheap Cash Store" replaced Jones' Apothecary Shop
and was itself eclipsed by an antique shop. This patrician view of the
scarcely bustling main intersection of town is afforded from the
balcony of Murphys' Hotel.

Whether he came by land or by sea, the typical 49'er was exhausted and nearly broke by the time he reached California. And he was in for some surprises. Our hero soon discovered that making his way from San Francisco to the mines—whether by riverboat, stagecoach, or foot—was an ordeal in itself. Once there, he was astonished by unbelievable prices ($3 for one egg) and wildly overcrowded hotels and boarding houses featuring straw mattresses only two feet wide. His naive inquiries about where to look for the precious nuggets he'd heard of were greeted with cackles, free-floating rumors, and the plaintive song, "When I got there, the mining ground was staked and claimed for miles around."

Learning that "seeing the elephant" meant going after the gold, he went out to learn how it was done. As witnessed by one visitor to Hangtown in 1851: "Along the whole length of the creek, as far as one could see, on the banks of the creek, in the ravines, in the middle of the principal and only street of the town, and even inside some of the houses, were parties of miners, numbering from three or four to a dozen, all hard at work, some laying into it with picks, some shoveling the dirt into the 'long toms,' or with long-handled shovels washing the dirt thrown in, and throwing out the stones, while others were working pumps or bailing water out of the holes with buckets. There was a continual noise and clatter, as mud, dirt, stones, and water were thrown about in all directions; the men, dressed in ragged clothes and big boots, wielding picks and shovels, and rolling big rocks about, were all working as if for their lives. . . . "

VENERABLE TECHNIQUE of gold panning depends on the fact that gold is quite heavy. As the miner swirls water around in the pan, the worthless dirt spills out while the gold granules sink to the bottom.

TREASURES FROM THE EARTH:
HOW GOLD IS DEPOSITED

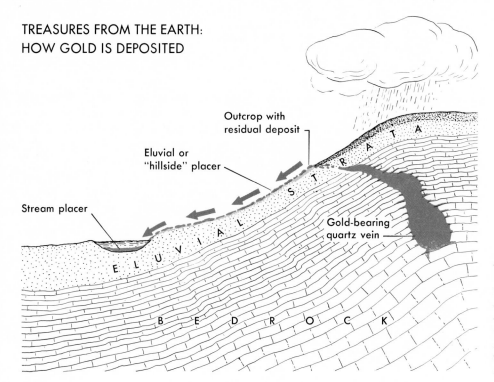

Outcrop with residual deposit

Eluvial or "hillside" placer

Stream placer

Gold-bearing quartz vein

S T R A T A

E L U V I A L

B E D R O C K

MOLTEN GOLD from deep in the earth flowed upward into fractures to form primary or vein deposits. As the earth's surface eroded, some veins were exposed as out-croppings. Further erosion disinte-grated the outcroppings, tumbling the gold particles down along the hills and into streams.

ANTHONY & BAKER SC.

VARIOUS MEANS of mining gold were depicted in this early letter-sheet. Below the idealized rendering was space on which the 49'ers wrote letters home.

COMPLETELY CUT OFF
from the lives they had known,
many young 49'ers poured out
their feelings of fear and isolation
in letters that would take many
months to reach their destinations.

Mining Camp Life: LONELINESS AND HILARITY

The typical young 49'er was forced to grow up in a hurry, but he did not easily get over feeling sorry for himself. Countless drawings show the footloose, bearded Argonaut alternately facing a bear in his tent, starving, dreaming of a wife, or struggling through the snow listening fearfully to the howl of wolves.

To combat loneliness and frustration, the miner lived it up when he could. After counting his "wages" (weighing his gold dust in a crude scale), he ventured forth from his tent, shanty, or boarding house and headed for the boom-town saloons. Ninety-two percent of California's population in 1850 was male, but the more prosperous camps featured "hurdy-gurdy girls" — pay-as-you-go dancing partners — and gaudy brothels.

Religion not being the most prevalent instinct, the towns' carnival atmosphere came to fullest flower on Sunday. The Argonaut thronged through the dusty, narrow streets, buying provisions, slapping old friends on the back, throwing away his hard-earned money at gaming tables, and watching horse races, bear-and-bull fights, or traveling variety shows.

On Sunday nights the barbers would work late, panning their careful sweeping of whiskers and hair cuttings for traces of gold. And thick-fingered bartenders—who, in receiving "pinches" of the miners' dust had let traces of it sift onto the floor— would go home and pan the mud that clung to their shoes.

HOPE OR DISAPPOINTMENT? A little of both, perhaps, in the face of Argonaut Solomon Yeakel, who spruced himself up for this tiny portrait—perhaps to send to his family "back in the States."

ROISTERING FUN of miners at play was illustrated vividly, if somewhat sentimentally, in Century Magazine. When no women were available, the men sometimes took turns as dancing partners. Not shown here was the custom of tying a bandana around the arm of the "ladies."

COPPEROPOLIS, CALIFORNIA
TOWN WITH A TARNISHED PAST

a GHOST TOWN worth seeing

From Stockton, go one mile south on U.S. 50, turn left on State 4, go thirty-seven miles east over this winding, hilly, scenic road to Copperopolis. Alternatively, from Angels Camp, on State 49, go southwest thirteen miles on State 4.

Suddenly, California copper flared into prominence. In 1863 alone, 380 new copper companies issued stock to excited California investors, who failed to see that the commodity's inflated price of 55¢ a pound was based on transitory factors: protective tariffs, unusually low ocean freight rates, and the Civil War's demand for shells and bullets. When local smelting proved impracticable, the raw ore was sent by sailing ship all the way around Cape Horn to the East Coast and to England. Then the War ended. Freight rates from California escalated. The world's copper supplies swelled. When the price plummeted to 19¢, California copper went out of business as quickly as it had come in.

Copperopolis, the center of all the activity, withered and died. Its long spur railroad was never even finished. The defunct mining companies left their headframes jutting like phantoms into the silent sky; and today, a hundred years later, they're still there. So are several of the abandoned buildings, including the Civil War armory of the Copperopolis Blues. Built partly of bricks hauled over from Columbia, where the frenetic miners were tearing down buildings in order to mine the ground under them, this staunch survivor is famous for its iron doors, which may be the largest in the Mother Lode.

The hills and countryside around Copperopolis also contain various sun-baked remnants, including a long, and very old, stone fence along Highway 4, west of town.

FORGOTTEN FIELDS around Copperopolis are strewn with the weathered remains of many eras, many enterprises. Demise of this old piece of farming equipment is measured by the weeds threading their way through its seams and sprockets.

LEFT BEHIND in the collapse of Copperopolis' copper industry were a number of gaunt mining structures. This one, the headframe of the Copper Consolidated Mining Company, broods over the center of the scanty town.

WHO LIVED in this old house? No one seems to remember. But if you prowl through it, you can find round nails indicating a later vintage than Copperopolis' squat stone edifices, which date back to the 1860's.

The Hydraulickers: RISE AND FALL OF AN UPSTART BREED

Figuring this land was their land, they tapped the water power of the mighty Sierra and aimed it at California's hills. Their high-pressure nozzles poured $270 million dollars of "color" into the sluice boxes—a sixth of the gold ever mined in the state—and washed away more dirt than was excavated from the Panama Canal.

AWESOME DISPLAY of the power of hydraulic mining was recorded in this view of the Malakoff Diggins, near Nevada City. Here as elsewhere, a torrent of debris clogged rivers, caused floods, and ruined farmlands until, in 1884, the practice was legally abolished. By attracting out-of-work miners up and down the gold country, hydraulicking created new camps which, in turn, became ghost towns (see following page).

FROM THE COOL GLOOM under the boardwalk roof of North Bloomfield's general store, you look out at an old firehouse, bell, and other mementoes of the town's golden era. Strictly speaking, North Bloomfield is not a true ghost town, because there are still a few residents. But the atmosphere is one of ghostly abandonment.

NORTH BLOOMFIELD, CALIFORNIA
IN HYDRAULICKINGS' SHADOW

"Humbug!" somebody grunted, and the disappointed Argonauts figured it wasn't a bad name for the town itself. Some wandering, drunken miner had raved about all the rich gold to be found around the place, but when the experienced prospectors got there they found the deposits too low-grade to work. That was in 1851.

In the 70's things were different. The town had been appropriately rechristened, and the low-grade gravels were succumbing to the fantastic new method known as hydraulicking (see pp. 31-2). Now thousands of men were earning good wages erecting and maintaining the hundreds of miles of canals and flumes that channeled the water down from the High Sierra reservoirs. Many others operated the long lines of sluices, whose design was improved until they became one of the most efficient gold recovery systems in California. The mine was huge and rich; the North Bloomfield Gravel Mining Company shipped one bar of pure gold that weighed 510 pounds.

The town prospered. Then in 1884, after a bitter counterattack by farmers and other residents of the lower valleys, whose lands and rivers were being wrecked by hydraulicking, a U.S. Court prohibited the Company from dumping tailings into the State's water arteries. This injunction effectively killed hydraulic mining in California.

It also killed North Bloomfield. A picturesque little ghost town today, it should be seen in tandem with a visit to the Malakoff Diggins, whose weirdly eroded cliffs are the best surviving example of the ecological nightmare of hydraulic mining.

From Auburn, on Interstate 80, take State 49 twenty-nine miles north to Nevada City, turn left to stay on State 49 for about a mile west, then go northeast on the "North Bloomfield Road," which makes hairpin turns through more than fifteen miles of rugged, forested mountains before reaching the town.

a GHOST TOWN worth seeing

AS IF MUSING on bygone years, a figure dressed in a century-old wedding dress stands poised in the window of North Bloomfield's general store, which has long been closed to business.

The scarcity of women during the gold rush gave them an added value, often redeemable in cash. In December of 1849 one of the early Argonauts wrote, "To give an idea how scarce women were, I will mention that when our vessel came into the harbor, we were boarded by half a dozen or more boats, and they all inquired if there were any women on board; they would give them two or three hundred dollars to sit behind a gambling table or fill some similar position." At a time when California's population was 90% male, the gamblers happily paid "an ounce" ($16) for the privilege of sitting near a girl at the tables, and the price ran as high as $600 for a whole night's companionship.

The earliest women to arrive in any number came from Mexico and Latin America. Sonoran miners were unique in bringing their entire families with them for the overland migration, and then in returning home to Mexico each winter. In 1851, the town of Sonora, California was reported to have as many women as men. But from the abjectly poor seaports of Mexico, Central America, and South America came boatloads of female slaves. Outnumbering the males at home, they paid no fare and were either auctioned off on arrival, or indentured to the ship's captain for half their earnings as laundresses, prostitutes, and gamblers' lures.

Yet there were many varieties of feminine enterprise. As early as June 20, 1848, a San Francisco journalist wrote, "An American woman, who had recently established a boarding-house here, pulled up stakes, and was off before her lodgers had even time to pay their bills." She presumably resumed her profession in the gold region, as others were doing. One of these admitted with remarkable candor that "Every man thought every woman a beauty. Even I have had men come forty miles over the mountains just to look at me, and I never was called a handsome woman, in my best days, even by my most ardent admirers."

Not all the stories, however, were happy ones. It was apparently a young widow who wrote home to her sister in 1853: "I am in a publick house to work I am not able to do very harde worke but can make forty of fifty dollars pr month I have been able to earn wages but a short time. . . . I am very loonly much to dishearten me but I have meny warm friends I have numbers of chances to change my name I may change it if can get one that will be kind to me as I am aloan. Thommy is gone he was my all I am now aloan oh Sister P . . ."

Other tales are less poignant. One adventuress disguised herself as a man, changed her name to "Old Charlie," and became one of California's best-known stage coach drivers. Another — the first woman to arrive in Nevada City in 1849— supplemented her husband's income by selling dried-apple pies for a dollar apiece every Sunday. Since the supply was limited, the miners would crowd around her door, gambling at euchre to decide who would be lucky enough to buy Mrs. Phelps' famous pies. And in Rich Bar, an old prospector, who noticed that one of the town's three female residents was earning $100 a week taking in laundry, commented: "Such women ain't common, I tell you; if they were, a man might marry and make money by the operation."

SEIZING ON BIZARRE doings in California as a source of humor, eastern magazines presented scenes like this, in which "A charming girl of New York," armed with pistol and sword, urges her captive Argonaut to dig harder for gold.

A WOMAN'S PRESENCE was highly prized. This lady appears to be holding a basket: perhaps she has brought the miners their lunch. In 1852, such an event would indeed have merited sending for the nearest photographer.

WIVES AND DAUGHTERS
of early California miners
had to be strong to adapt
to a rough-and-ready man's
world. Top: Emma Johnson,
daughter of a Hangtown
miner. Below: a miner's
widow mourns his death.

SONG-AND-DANCE STAR
Lotta Crabtree (above) was
trained and launched by
Lola Montez at the age of 7.
An overnight success, she
left Grass Valley to travel
throughout the gold country
and on to international fame.

Tracking down vanished mining camps? Look for fruit trees. Many a pioneer housewife—whether she came jolting across the plains or bobbing around the Horn—brought along little bags of seeds to help civilize and feed the new communities.

Especially in the rugged terrain of the Northern mines, food supplies could be chancy; the lack of fresh fruit, vegetables, and other staples was a constant threat to health. Wrote housewife Shirley Clappe to her sister, "We have had no fresh meat for nearly a month! Dark and ominous rumors are also floating through the moist air, to the effect that the potatoes and onions are about to give out! But don't be alarmed, dear Molly. There is no danger of famine. For have we not got wagon loads of hard, dark hams, whose indurated hearts nothing but the sharpest knife and the stoutest arm can penetrate? Have we not got quintals of dreadful mackerel, fearfully crystalized in black salt? Have we not barrels of rusty pork. . . ?"

Many pioneer housewives' implements can be seen in the gold country today. A typical kitchen might contain a Dutch oven, camp kettle, frying pan (called a "spider"), coffee pot, tin plates and cups, iron spoons, knives and forks, rolling pin, bread pan, and milk or water can. Butcher knives were scarce. If there were no baking pan, the housewife speared slices of bacon or rolls of bread dough on sharpened willow switches, then held them over the open fire.

One of Mrs. Clappe's friends had a stove so badly designed that "the soot sifted through in large quantities, and covered us from head to foot, and though I bathed so often that my hands were dreadfully chapped and bled profusely, from having them so much in the water, yet in spite of my efforts, I looked like a chimney-sweep, masquerading in women's clothes."

Caring for the little ones was no picnic, either. Mrs. Clappe wrote that "This is an awful place for children; and nervous mothers would 'die daily,' if they could see little Mary running fearlessly to the edge of, and looking down in these holes—many of them sixty feet in depth—which have been excavated in the hope of finding gold, and of course left open." Another journal relates that when the father was away, "Mother kept her children close to the home all day. When evening came, she tucked them in their beds very early, then making sure that the window and door were well barred, she set herself to the task of sewing or darning the numerous little stockings. Many times the brave woman, alone in the solitary house, sat and worked well into the night while her babes slept near her side. Often the wild panther screamed near the window or a hungry bear roamed back and forth in front of the cabin. The mother was always glad, at these times, when morning came, and with it the cheering rays of sunlight."

Despite the hardships, a zestful love of life in the new land can be read between the lines of almost all the letters. And as the camps matured, life improved. In her final correspondence from the gold fields, Mrs. Clappe is perfectly sincere in advising her sister, "Really, everybody ought to go to the mines, just to see how little it takes to make people comfortable in the world."

WORLDLY BEAUTY, Lola Montez in her twenties was the mistress and enchantress of Europe's most famous men of culture. At 35 she came to California, failed as a theatrical performer, and set up housekeeping in Grass Valley. Still restless and unhappy, she returned to Europe and then New York, where she died in 1861, at the age of 43. Framed portrait at far left shows her in her younger years; casual pose at near left, closer to her death.

Woman in Town! TOURISM'S MIDAS TOUCHES

Sleep in an antique bed, drink at a brass rail.
Go antiquing for silly souvenirs or the real thing.
Some of the old inns along Highway 49 have
won awards for their restored elegance.
Rough-and-ready—or impressively posh—the
gold country is golden again.

TAKE-AWAY TREASURES are plentiful in the antique shops of the gold rush towns. These shoppers carry their "finds" down the lovely main street of Amador City.

OLD INNS along Highway 49 vie with one another for the authenticity of their period decor. Both Georgetown's rustic Georgetown Hotel (bottom) and Sonora's fancier Gunn House (top) are done in Victorian style.

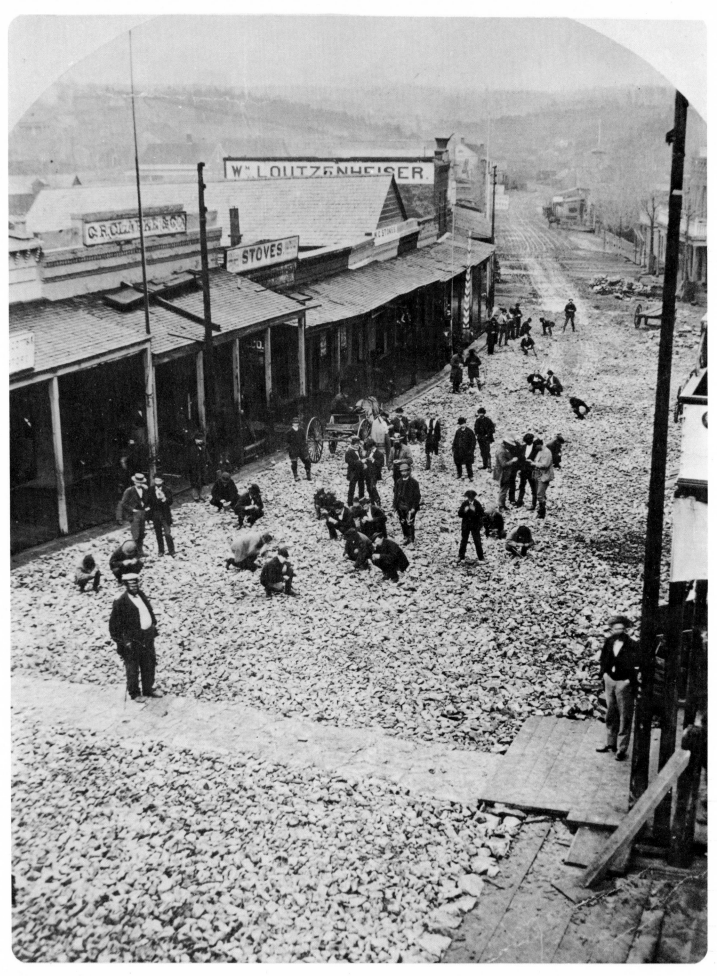

LITERALLY PAVED WITH GOLD when it was macadamized in 1873, Grass Valley's Main Street suddenly became the object of a frenetic search by grizzled miners looking for rocks containing a good grade of ore.

NEVADA CITY/GRASS VALLEY, CALIFORNIA
HARDROCK MINES BUILT GENTEEL COMMUNITIES

The term "ghost town" would have to be stretched very far to include Nevada City and Grass Valley. Yet these twins sum up the mature years of California gold mining. While the placer camps flared and fizzled, Nevada City and Grass Valley were taking root in the firmer soil of the industrial revolution. Their hardrock ores, crushed and melted in heavy machinery turned out by Nevada City's famous Miner's Foundry, supported a broadly-based economic development. Out of this grew these communities of astonishing grace and permanency.

Seeing them today, you sense that while Nevada City contributed the refinement, little, still-humming Grass Valley supplied more of the muscle. Grass Valley's gold mines—the Empire, Pennsylvania, North Star, Gold Center, and others—lie on the periphery of the town proper. Producing more than $100 million in just over a hundred years, they kept Grass Valley prosperous with a consistency unique in the West, even through the depression of the 1930's. Outside the well-organized little museum is an immense Pelton wheel, which efficiently transformed available water energy into rock-crushing power.

Nevada City's great attraction is her beauty. She speaks with a faint New England accent, and the seasons bring dramatic changes to her lush hillside lanes, her steeples, her venerable business buildings, and her wonderful old homes. As a final touch, the City Council voted in 1971 to install twenty-six gas lamps along Broad Street, to make Nevada perhaps the only town in America whose main thoroughfare is lighted by gas.

a GHOST TOWN worth seeing

From Auburn, on Interstate 80, take State 49 twenty-four miles north to Grass Valley; Nevada City is five miles farther on, to the northeast. Most drivers use the freeway, but the old road, just north of the freeway, is more scenic and less hurried.

HOLDING CANDLES to light their way through the underground darkness, miners descend into the tunnels of Grass Valley's Empire Mine.

FALL COLORS bring a crowning glory to the stately homes and churches of Nevada City and Grass Valley. Nowhere else in California are such Eastern architectural motifs as widow's walks, garden gazebos, picket fences, and mullioned windows found in such rich abundance, or tended with such loving care. Far left: Nevada City's Trinity Episcopal Church, opened in 1873. Left: Marsh house, on Boulder Street, Boulder Hill, Nevada City. Below, left: The Red Castle, now a hotel, on Prospect Hill, Nevada City. Below, right: Bourn mansion, near Empire Mine, Grass Valley. Bottom: house on Boulder Street, Boulder Hill, Nevada City.

MELLOWED WITH AGE, Forest's silent facades are hidden from the average tourist by their mountain-girt isolation. Along with such nearby camps as Allegheny and Goodyear's Bar, this ghost town experienced its brief but roaring heyday well over a hundred years ago.

WELL OFF the beaten track, Johnsville's ghostly buildings are the product of a gold boom that, by California standards, came relatively late—the 1870's. Once called Jamison, Johnsville is now part of Plumas-Eureka State Park, whose overseers plan to restore the old stamp mill and some of the other wooden structures.

Backroad Haunts: GHOSTS BEYOND HIGHWAY 49

Get off the main drag! The gold country's truest ghosts are on the smaller roads leading back into the hills. The breezy trees and buzzing locusts will welcome you; so will these somnolent communities, scarcely brushed by tourism, where time seems nearly to have stopped.

SLUMBERING IN A WOODED HOLLOW among the hills northeast of Jackson, Volcano was so named because its founders mistakenly believed the little valley to be an extinct volcanic crater. Opened in 1848, and reputedly producing nearly a hundred million dollars worth of gold bullion, Volcano was among the earliest and richest of California camps.

Old-Time Gaiety: GOLD COUNTRY FROLICS

Many's the fiesta that's been revived in California's gold rush country to recall the century when the forty-niners lived and played. If the sport's unorthodox, so much the better: When you make your own entertainment, you give it all you've got.

SPOUTING HOSES and panting firemen wrestling with antique equipment mark Columbia's Firemen's Muster, which is put on every spring.

FROG FANCIERS' finest hour comes in May at Angels Camp, when the Calaveras County Fair reenacts the frog jumping contest of Mark Twain's famous story.

FIDDLETOWN Fiddlers
Contest fiddles in a different
sense than was meant by
the old Missourian who gave
the town its name in 1849.
He was piqued by the
younger miners in his party,
who, he said, were "always
fiddling."

SPIRITED BIDDING lures all
the best white elephants out
of basement and barn to
the Annual Kit Carson
Mountain Men Auction in
Jackson each February.

NUGGET of tourist interest, the restored
Fallon House Theater presents live stage
performances. A repertory group of actors
spends the whole summer in Columbia, living
at picturesque Eagle Cottage, an old
boarding house just down the street.

ABSORBED in his next
urgent amusement, a spirited
young'un passes the well-kept
home of one of Columbia's few
full-time residents. The bunting is
out in honor of Fourth of July,
a peak day for this tourist town.

COLUMBIA, CALIFORNIA
DRESS UP OR DOWN, AND BRING THE KIDS

There's plenty to do in Columbia—stage coach rides, the ice cream parlor, gold panning, saloons, a serious theater, and more. Although it slumbered for nearly a century after having once been the Mother Lode's top mining camp, Columbia makes no pretense of being a true ghost town. Meticulously restored by the State Park people, the old brick buildings wear full commercial regalia—banners, fresh paint, and Ye Olde signs. Besides the tourists, who come in droves, there are a few full-time residents. You can see their mail in the ancient post-office boxes, or shop at the general store with them, or even sit in on a genuine legal proceeding at the Main Street courthouse.

Like so many of the truer ghosts, Columbia teems with history. Her flat valley is blessed with a unique geological formation: a limestone bed, full of potholes which caught and held the gold flakes that washed down from the surrounding hills over thousands of years. Thus, the topsoil proved exceedingly rich, yielding—according to one estimate—about $87 million. In the early 1850's her fifteen thousand or more residents made Columbia the second or third largest city in California, with forty saloons and gambling halls, seventeen general stores, eight hotels, three churches, three theaters, two fire companies, and four banks.

From Manteca, on U.S. 50, take State 120/108 fifty-five miles east to Sonora. Then turn left, go seven miles northwest to Columbia. Sonora itself contains interesting gold rush mementos, as do Jamestown and Chinese Camp.

a GHOST TOWN worth seeing

CROWD PLEASING is Columbia's stock-in-trade, and that includes dancing in the street as well as loud shoot-outs, ragtime piano players in the saloons, stage coach rides, and red garter girls.

Shasta's Shadows: RETRACING CALIFORNIA'S NORTHERN GOLD RUSH

Above the Sacramento Valley lay a gold region
that was in many ways the wildest of them all. Less
publicized than the Mother Lode and Northern
Mines, these boom camps clung to their rough-and-
tumble ways longer. But here, too,
the gold ran out, and one camp after the next
had to close its swinging doors.

*LONGEST ROW of brick
structures in California
was what the town boosters
claimed for Shasta in the
1850's. They were put up
to prevent another holocaust
such as leveled the camp's
frame-built center in 1853,
remain as the chief memento
of early-day Shasta.*

COURT'S COME TO ORDER, *thanks to the restorer's art, in the old mining town of Shasta, whose rowdy habits once gave the judge plenty to worry about. Shasta's golden wealth and lonely isolation were tailor-made for outlaws with names like Rattlesnake Dick and Sheet-Iron Jack.*

VARIED MEMORIES *flicker in the silent shadows of this gold-rush ghost at Helena, California. Downstairs the stone-and-brick edifice housed a brewery, while the upstairs apparently served as a school by day and a brothel by night.*

Golden Gate Ghosts: SPRITES OF THE BAY AREA

Strange to say, there are ghost towns within
the immediate orbit of the San Francisco Bay
Area. "Old" New Almaden, south of San Jose,
is one; another is China Camp, south of Santa
Cruz. But the most surprising survivor is
right on San Francisco Bay.

*DOZING ON A MUD FLAT laced with catwalks
is Drawbridge, one of the West's most
unusual ghost towns. Built about 1880
as a duck-hunting and gambling retreat,
Drawbridge hit its peak during the roaring
twenties, when special trains hauled in
hundreds of good-timers every weekend.
But the Depression killed the town. To reach
Drawbridge, go to Alviso (near San Jose),
then walk out two miles along the railroad
tracks jutting into the Bay. But look out for the
locomotive, and be advised
that this is private property.*

RELIC OF HOLLYWOOD films as well as of primitive fire-fighting days, this mobile steam engine is one of a collection of old vehicles at Burton's Tropico Gold Mine, north of Lancaster in the Antelope Valley.

A CHANCE to dress up in old-time outfits is one of the attractions of Calico, a commercial ghost town near Barstow, in the Mojave Desert.

CROWD COMFORTS and make-believe mysteries worthy of Disneyland are the goals of hundreds of Southern California pleasure seekers who pass many miles of open desert country every weekend to reach Walter Knott's tourist mecca of Calico.

Southern California: SHOW-BIZ GHOST TOWNS

Gold lamé is okay, and real Hollywood cowboys
patrol the boardwalks, shooting off their blanks.
There's sarsaparilla aplenty, and the haunted houses
are rated GP. Short on ghosts but long on tourists,
Southern California has conjured
up some bonanza camps of its own.

Southern California: GHOSTS OF THE GREAT DESERTS

Each year, as Southern California's population continues to swell—and as back-road vehicles become increasingly popular—more and more people explore the fascinating deserts to the east. Here the air and ground are clean, the scenery dramatic, and the wide-open, sixteen-million-acre space seemingly unbounded.

With the explosive growth of desert tourism, the far-flung ghost towns, along with many other unspoiled features, have inevitably suffered. Yet, for lovers of the off-the-beaten-track, they're still well worth exploring.

The typical Mojave ghost town is not extensive. It sprang up in lonely isolation, rather than as part of the powerful historical trend which swept the Mother Lode towns into existence. When the ore gave out, the camp died fast. This barren land offered no further way for anyone to make a living, and as citizens abandoned the town almost as quickly as they had come, it became a far purer ghost than its elder counterparts to the north. Less substantial in the first place, the untended buildings and artifacts were soon ravaged by sun, wind, rain, and—eventually—vandals. In many cases, the heavy mining equipment is all that has lasted. Scour the hillsides and valleys in the vicinity of the townsite, but beware of open or concealed mine shafts, especially if you take children or pets along.

For a guide to the best of these stark old settlements, see page 61. Avid seekers of the vanished or near-vanished camps may consult Remi Nadeau's *Ghost Towns and Mining Camps of California* and the monthly features in *Desert Magazine*.

STAGE COACH STATION on the old Butterfield Overland Mail Line is at Vallecito, between the Tierra Blanca Mountains and the western edge of Anza Borrego State Park. Opened in 1858, the famous stage line carried mail and passengers 2,630 miles from Tipton, Missouri, to El Paso, Tucson, Los Angeles, and San Francisco in about 22 days.

SOURDOUGH PANCAKES and eggs taste great in the fresh Mojave air. Back-road vehicles and camping on your own are features of ghost-towning in Southern California's deserts.

IMMENSE ORE BUCKETS are at Vanderbilt, a ghost town near the Nevada border, south of Las Vegas. The lady is Miss Nell Murbarger, queen of ghost town writers, who has published more than a thousand articles on the subject.

FOREST (Northeast of Sacramento; from State 49 north of Nevada City, either (a) paved road northeast from just north of Yuba River, or (b) dirt road south from Goodyears Bar). Not a pure ghost, but as close to one as can be found west of the Sierra. Forest flourished only briefly in the 1850's, and many of its deserted buildings date from later years. Scattered over hillsides among the evergreens are an interesting graveyard, a tobacco shop, a broken-down Catholic church, and brooding, empty houses. Before prowling through the latter, however, get permission from the caretaker, who lives next to the church.

VOLCANO (East of Sacramento, east of Jackson on State 88, then, at Pine Grove, 4 mi. north on secondary road). One of the oldest and quietest of the Mother Lode's semi-ghosts. The first of a whole series of towns which sprang up after gold was discovered here by U.S. troops in 1849, Volcano outlasted such colorful neighbors as Whiskey Slide, Loafer Flat, Bedbug, Hogtown, Helltown, and Murderer's Gulch. The town is well preserved. The quaint St. George Hotel still welcomes guests; other structures vary, from the still serviceable to mere crumbling shells. Don't miss the church and two cemeteries on the hill above town. Rolling, forested hill country.

AUBURN, JACKSON, JAMESTOWN, MARIPOSA, SONORA (All on State 49 except Jamestown which is 1 mi. east). Relatively large non-ghosts dating from the gold rush, containing many fine remnants of the period. Outstanding structures include Auburn's Old Town, County Courthouse, and striped firehouse; Jackson's Brown House, National Hotel, Kennedy Mine, and Serbian Orthodox Church (see photo); Jamestown's Emporium; Mariposa's jail, main street buildings, and County Courthouse; and Sonora's St. James Episcopal Church, I.O.O.F. Hall, and City Hotel. Excellent highway through oak-studded Sierra foothills; often hot in summer.

GHOST TOWNS IN THE SANTA CRUZ MOUNTAINS (South of San Jose; *New Almaden*, west off U.S. 101 just south of Coyote, 14 mi. south of San Jose; and *China Camp*, in the Forest of the Nisene Marks State Park, Aptos exit off State 1 about 7 mi. southeast of Santa Cruz, on Aptos Creek Road). New Almaden is California's earliest mining town; its mercury, known to the Indians, and mined by the Spanish after 1824, became valuable in the extraction of hard-rock gold ores after 1849. Main remnants are a schoolhouse, cemetery, and mining artifacts. China Camp's several structures are divided among high and low settlements, and an isolated superintendent's house (see photo). Several hours' hike through unmarked forest are needed; get directions from local Rangers.

HORNITOS (East of Modesto; west of Mariposa, off State 49 at Mt. Bullion on Hornitos Road). A standout among many small, somnolent semi-ghosts on or near Highway 49. Once frequented by notorious outlaw Joaquin Murrieta, Hornitos was one of the rowdiest of the early whoopee towns. Founded by Sonorans, it shows their influence more than any other California ghost, especially in its Mexican-style central plaza, around which cluster several typically low, iron-shuttered buildings.

California

HELENA, SHASTA, AND FRENCH GULCH (East of Eureka; Helena is 16 mi. west of Weaverville on State 299; Shasta, 6 mi. west of Redding on State 299; French Gulch north off State 299 from a point about 13 mi. west of Shasta). A trio of ghosts that survived "California's second gold rush"—the Trinity-Shasta boom, which began in 1849. Weaverville itself, while certainly no ghost, is full of historic structures, including an elaborately reconstructed Chinese Joss House. To spot little-known Helena, keep a sharp lookout to the north as the highway crosses the Trinity. Respect the petite town's quiet charm, and its present owner will prove friendly. French Gulch, while more alive, is nonetheless somnolent, and displays some fine old brick and wooden buildings, including the church (see photo). Shasta played a major role in the early days, is still a living town but includes such captivating oldies as long rows of brick ruins, a museum, a courthouse, a jail, a Masonic Hall, and a fine graveyard.

MOKELUMNE HILL (Southeast of Sacramento, on State 49 south of Sutter Creek). A fine, old, partial ghost analogous to Volcano or Murphys. Born in 1849, "Mok Hill" lived through one of the most violent heydays of any of the early towns, including a war between French and Yankee prospectors and an alleged murder every weekend for 17 weeks. From crumbling ruins to Highway 49's oldest surviving three-story building, Mok Hill includes an assortment of authentic structures; among them is the Hotel Leger, built in 1852 and now famed for its beautiful restoration and gourmet cooking.

JOHNSVILLE (Northwest of Reno; west off U.S. 395 on State 70; southwest of Blairsden on State A-14). One of the gold country's most remote and unusual partial ghosts. Built almost entirely of wood by an English mining company in the 1870's, Johnsville today consists of a few small, picturesquely preserved buildings; a couple of massive, boarded-up wrecks with overhanging balconies; some collapsing dwellings; and, off the main street, a number of spruced-up vacation homes. Plumas-Eureka State Park, in which the town is located, also maintains a little museum of mining artifacts. Green, partially forested countryside.

GHOST TOWNS OF THE SOUTHERN CALIFORNIA DESERTS (*Calico*, just east of Barstow, 3 mi. north of U.S. 15; *Burton's Tropico Mine and Gold Camp*, at Rosamond, north of Palmdale on State 14; *Randsburg*, northwest of Barstow on U.S. 395; *Ivanpah*, south of Las Vegas, Nev., west from U.S. 15 near the State Line at Yates Well, then several dirt roads and a walk—inquire locally and do not confuse with South Ivanpah, which is shown on road maps as Ivanpah; *Vanderbilt*, 4 mi. east of South Ivanpah along an old railroad bed in the New York Mountains; *Providence*, west of Needles, 25 mi. northwest of U.S. 66 at Essex in Mitchell Caverns State Park; *Dale*, 19 mi. east of Twenty Nine Palms on continuation of State 62—this is "Old Dale," "New Dale" and surrounding mines are 6 mi. southeast on a dirt road). Calico and Burton's (see photo) are rebuilt, restored towns with elaborate tourist facilities; the others are the best available remnants of the region's scattered mining booms of the late 19th and early 20th centuries. (For the ghost towns of east-central California, see Chapter 2.)

HURRYING TO CASH IN on the new bonanzas, the "boomers" built one instant town after the next across the bleak deserts of Nevada, eastern California, and western Utah. Shown here is the main street of Goldfield, Nevada, in 1904. Soon after, Goldfield entered a steep decline and joined many other mining camps of the Great Basin in heading toward ghost town status.

2

GREAT BASIN
HOORAH FOR WASHOE!
1859...

BY THE LATE FIFTIES, the California miners were restless— almost desperate. The easy pickings were gone. Footloose and disorderly, they constituted a veritable army of get-rich-quick types who wanted, not jobs, but a new bonanza. And suddenly there was one. Electrifying news came from across the Sierra: someone named Comstock had given his name to a fabulous silver strike!

As the prospectors raced for the new territory, famous Virginia City was born, yielding overnight fortunes that shortly outstripped even California's. And the curtain went up on one of the most astonishing scenarios in the history of the West: a whole series of lesser bonanzas and *borrascas* (busts) sweeping across the Great Basin—that vast, sagebrush wilderness rimmed by the Sierra Navada range, on the west, and Utah's Wasatch Mountains, to the east. Wave after raucous wave of humanity invaded the arid fastnesses, extending the cycle of wealth and disappointment well into the twentieth century. When the fickle hordes gave up at last, the dust of their departure filtered down on some of the ghostliest ghost towns anywhere.

More than one ghost was conceived in the strange events which preceded the discovery of the Comstock Lode. In a ravine leading down from the future Virginia City's Mt. Davidson, some California-bound miners had noticed traces of gold as early as 1849. The original finders did not tarry; but here, not long after, others founded the boomville of Silver City, Nevada. To the southwest, Mormon farmers had already established the Territory's first community of Genoa. When some of them abandoned an irrigation project to try gold mining, the little towns of Dayton and Johntown came into being.

But it remained for two Irishmen—Peter O'Riley and Patrick McLaughlin—to discover some black dirt and "blasted blue stuff" that proved the outcropping of a silver vein. In the twenty years following the first news of this bonanza, Virginia City and Gold Hill poured forth silver as well as gold to the tune of some three hundred million dollars.

The impact was felt far beyond "Washoe," as the territory was called. Much of the wealth found its way to San Francisco, where an important financial and banking system grew up around the frenzied trading of Comstock shares; Virginia silver virtually underwrote the diversified growth of this fancy new city-by-the-Golden Gate. The Comstock's factory-like atmosphere marked the first true industrial expansion in the West; as technological precedent and prototype, its influence was pervasive. And Washoe's sudden growth caused ripples in Washington, where Lincoln's government, drained by the Civil War and anxious for support in passing the Emancipation Proclamation, hurried the territory into statehood in 1864, rechristening it "Nevada."

In seeking out these depopulated mining camps, it is helpful to bear in mind the overall topography of the Great Basin, which is an immense, arid sink, ribbed by north-south mountain chains. Generally, the old camps are found near the lower slopes of the mountains. Since eastern California, Nevada, and western Utah are still very thinly populated, it's well, before you go, to remember the comment of an exasperated prospector named Mark Twain: "No flowers grow here, and no green thing gladdens the eye. The birds that fly over the land carry their provisions with them."

✕ **True Ghost Town:** Majority of buildings disused; few if any residents; no modern facilities.

✳ **Partial Ghost Town:** Some disused buildings; some residents; limited facilities.

★ **Tourist Ghost Town:** Old structures refurbished to promote old-time atmosphere; modern facilities.

🛡40 Interstate Highways

🛡80 U.S. Highways

95 State Highways & Secondary Roads

NOTE: Map is as accurate as present information permits. Refer to detailed maps for minor roads, and always inquire locally about road conditions.

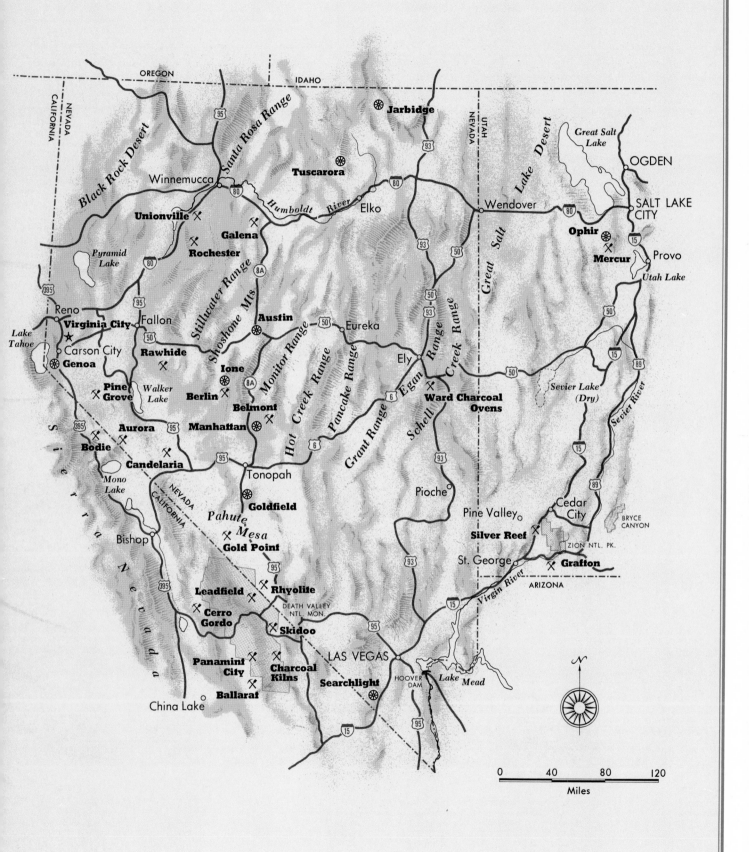

VIRGINIA CITY, NEVADA
"ALL IS LIFE, EXCITEMENT, AVARICE, LUST, DEVILTRY..."

a GHOST TOWN worth seeing

From Reno, go nine miles south on U.S. 395 to State 17, which rises steeply into the barren mountains to the southeast, reaching Virginia City in fourteen miles.

Perhaps the key to Virginia City's attraction today is that, though bustling tourism has replaced mining as the principal enterprise, the town's essential spirit is not all that different from what it was over a hundred years ago, when J. Ross Browne wrote, "Perhaps there is not another spot upon the face of the globe that presents a scene so weird and desolate in its natural aspect, yet so replete with busy life, so animate with human interest . . . saloons are glittering with their gaudy bars and fancy glasses and many-colored liquors, and thirsty men are swilling the burning poison; bill stickers are sticking up bills of auctions, theatres and new saloons . . . A strange city truly, abounding in strange exhibitions and startling combinations of the human passions." Yesteryear's highwaymen have given way to today's one-armed bandits, the great old mansions have turned into museums, and you're invited to tour some of those same mines where "a wondrous battle raged, in which the combatants were man and earth."

Open-season in Virginia City is from spring to fall. The biggest crowds, of course, come on weekends. But since few visitors stay overnight, you can beat even the summer throng by arriving in the early morning. Then, in the bright, shuttered silence, significant details can more easily catch one's eye, and the stolid buildings seem more willing to admit their age. Caught with its tinseled guard down, Virginia seems almost real.

MAVERICK atmosphere along Virginia City's main drag is a replay of the days when sweating miners rubbed elbows with silver barons, card sharks, and parlor ladies.

CENTURY-OLD SURVIVORS of Virginia's youth invite perusal before the midday crowds arrive. On weekend evenings in summer, variety shows are performed in the old Miners' Union Hall.

RED HOT MAMMAS belt out the good old numbers in variety shows at the former Miners' Union Hall. The tongue-in-cheek melodramas are innocent by twentieth century standards, and children are welcome.

BUCKET OF BLOOD, one of the best-known saloons in Virginia City, features Victorian decor, ragtime-and-washboard music, and slot machines.

MOST AUTHENTICALLY furnished of the town's several mansions, "The Castle" remains as it was in boom times. Its three successive owners have carefully kept such features as 150-year-old Czechoslovakian crystal chandeliers, hand-blocked wallpaper from France, and Comstock silver doorknobs.

SQUARE-SET TIMBERING:
THE CRUCIAL LINK

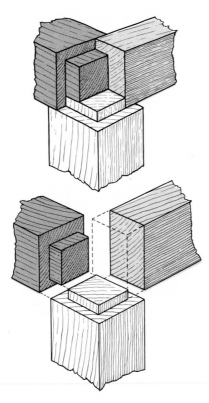

MAJOR ADVANCE in mining technology made on the Comstock was a basically simple method called "square-set timbering." Mortise-and-tenon joints (above) locked timber ends together, and timbers formed an endless series of hollow cribs four by six feet square, as in mine at right. Such a honeycomb could reinforce larger underground cavities than could single timbers, and the structure could be made stronger yet by filling vertical columns with waste rock.

EXTERIOR OF THE HOISTING WORKS

WORKING THE LEDGE

BIGGEST PRODUCER of all on Nevada's Comstock was the famous Belcher Mine, which churned out over $26 million worth of silver and gold between 1863 and 1916. Belcher stock bolstered the Comstock financial craze by zooming from $1.50 a share in 1870 to $1,525 a share nineteen months later. Square set timbering enabled the mine to reach great depths, where the rock was so hot that despite "the only air-shaft on the Comstock lode worthy of the name," the men were able to work only in very brief shifts before returning to higher levels to cool off.

INDUSTRIALIZATION OF THE WEST began in Virginia City, Nevada. This picture, taken in the 1870's, shows the famous Hale and Norcross mill in the foreground. The town proper is partly obscured by atmospheric pollution, which Virginia City also introduced to the West.

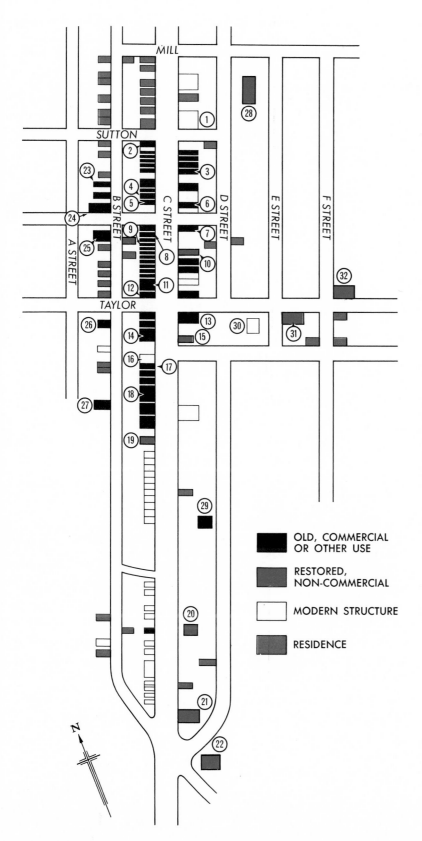

VIRGINIA CITY, NEVADA, 1971

1. The Way it Was Museum
2. Comstock Assay Office Museum
3. Brass Rail Saloon
4. Silver Queen Saloon and Hotel
5. IOOF Hall and Historical Museum
6. Silver Dollar Hotel
7. Bucket of Blood Saloon
8. Delta Saloon
9. Visitors' Bureau
10. Territorial Enterprise
11. Red Garter Saloon
12. Crystal Bar
13. Mark Twain Museum (Museum of Memories)
14. Old Washoe Club
15. Old Fire House (now Town Hall)
16. Post Office
17. Old 62 Bar
18. 1859 Boarding House Exhibit and Prison Museum
19. Presbyterian Church
20. Savage House
21. Fourth-Ward School
22. Chollar Mansion
23. Miners' Union Hall
24. Pipers ·Opera
25. Storey County Court House
26. Pioneer Livery
27. The Castle
28. V and T Freight Depot
29. Mackay House
30. School
31. St. Mary's in the Mountains Catholic Church
32. St. Paul's Episcopal Church

OLD, COMMERCIAL OR OTHER USE

RESTORED, NON-COMMERCIAL

MODERN STRUCTURE

RESIDENCE

Grandiose Residue: COMSTOCK SCHEMES

In an era when the fantastic became commonplace, nobody seemed surprised by sundry immodest proposals put forward by men of purportedly logical mind for taming the rich but recalcitrant earth. Workable or not, some of the more colossal results are still with us.

TO SOLVE simultaneously the problems of flooding, intense heat, and ore transport encountered by the deep Comstock mines, Adolph Sutro (left) in 1865 proposed digging a horizontal ventilating tunnel from the Carson Valley, four miles away. At great expense, and after many complications, the tunnel (below) was completed in 1878. But by then the ore had almost given out, and the scheme never paid for itself—though it paid Sutro, who sold his stock early. Near the tunnel mouth is the little ghost town of Sutro.

MAMMOTH remains of a richly financed but ill-fated plan to reprocess Comstock tailings are sprawled across American Flat, which can be reached via a short dirt road heading west from Gold Hill, just south of Virginia City, Nevada.

SAMUEL CLEMENS came West with his brother in 1861 and later wrote Roughing It, a marvelously funny book about his journey and his impressions of Virginia City. As an unlucky prospector in the Esmeralda District of Nevada, he sent Virginia City's Territorial Enterprise humorous sketches which he signed "Josh." Hired by the paper for $25 a week, he stayed with it for two years, signing his columns "Mark Twain" (see column at right) and perfecting the style that would soon earn him worldwide acclaim.

TERRITORIAL ENTERPRISE

Wednesday --- April 25, 1866

A SONG.

BY GEORGE ARNOLD.

O, cool, green waves, that ebb and flow,
  Reflecting calm, blue skies above,
How gently now ye come and go,
  Since you have drowned my love.

Ye lap the shore of beaten sand,
  With cool, salt ripples circling by;
But from your depths a ghostly hand
  Points upward to the sky.

O waves! strew corals, white and red,
  With shells and strange weeds from the deep,
To make a rare and regal bed
  Whereon my love may sleep.

May sleep, and sleeping, dream of me
  In dreams that lovers find so sweet;
And I will couch me by the sea
  That we in dreams may meet.

LETTER FROM MARK TWAIN.

[Correspondence of the Sacramento Union.]
HONOLULU, March, 1866.

COMING HOME FROM PRISON.

I am probably the most sensitive man in the kingdom of Hawaii to-night—especially about sitting down in the presence of my betters. I have ridden fifteen or twenty miles on horseback since 5 P. M., and to tell the honest truth, I have a delicacy about sitting down at all. I am one of the poorest horsemen in the world, and I never mount a horse without experiencing a sort of dread that I may be setting out on that last mysterious journey which all of us must take sooner or later, and I never come back in safety from a horseback trip without thinking of my latter end for two or three days afterward. This same old regular devotional sentiment began just as soon as I sat down here five minutes ago.

An excursion to Diamond Head and the King's Cocoanut Grove was planned to-day —time, 4:30 P. M.—the party to consist of half a dozen gentlemen and three ladies. They all started at the appointed hour except myself. I was at the Government Prison, and got so interested in its examination that I did not notice how quickly the time was passing. Somebody remarked that it was twenty minutes past 5 o'clock, and that woke me up. It was a fortunate circumstance that Captain Phillips was there with his "turn-out," as he calls a top-buggy that Captain Cook brought here in 1778, and a horse that was here when Captain Cook came. Captain Phillips takes a just pride in his driving and in the speed of his horse, and to his passion for displaying them I owe it that we were only sixteen minutes coming from the prison to the American Hotel—a distance which has been estimated to be over half a mile. But it took some awful driving. The Captain's whip came down fast, and the blows started so much dust out of the horse's hide that during the last half of the journey we rode through an impenetrable fog, and ran by a pocket compass in the hands of Captain Fish, a whaler Captain of twenty-six years experience, who sat there through that perilous voyage as self-possessed as if he had been on the euchre-deck of his own ship, and calmly said, "Port your helm—port," from time to time, and "Hold her a little free—steady—so-o," and "Luff—hard down to starboard!" and never once lost his presence of mind or betrayed the least anxiety by voice or manner. When we came to anchor at last, and Captain Phillips looked at his watch and said, "Sixteen minutes—I told you it was in her! that's over three miles an hour!" I could see he felt entitled to a compliment, and so I said I had never seen lightning go like that horse. And I never had.

THE STEED "OAHU."

The landlord of the American said the party had been gone nearly an hour, but that he could give me my choice of several horses that could easily overtake them. I said, never mind—I preferred a safe horse to a fast one—I would like to have an excessively gentle horse—a horse with no spirit whatever—a lame one, if he had such a thing. Inside of five minutes I was mounted, and perfectly satisfied with my outfit. I had no time to label him "This is a horse," and so if the public took him for a sheep I cannot help it. I was satisfied, and that was the main thing. I could see that he had as many fine points as any man's

The Boardwalk Press: THE FACTS AND OTHER NEWS

Much of the verve and color of the exploding West was captured by its newspapers, which not only described events but became, in themselves, part of the wonderfully wild scene.

In the Great Basin, as elsewhere, upstart papers shared many problems. The hand-operated presses were primitive at best. Oftener than not, the editor was also the printer and business manager—a combination of talents not always happily wedded in one personality. Again and again the early sheets cried out for financial help, in cash or in kind. "We can't publish without paper; please send us your rags!" wailed Utah's *Deseret News,* which went on to request wheat, corn, butter, calves, pigs, and the furs of beaver, otter, mink, wolf, or fox. One editor simply gave up and committed suicide; another stole a grave marker and made a printer's stone out of it. Every paper had a vital stake in the longevity and prosperity of its community, and plumped it hard while ridiculing rival papers and towns.

The miners, in their isolated settlements, were hungry for news from "back East"— and vitally interested in fast-breaking developments in gold and silver prospecting. Highly prone to rumor themselves, they were fussy neither about factual accuracy nor about grammar or spelling: what they wanted was excitement.

Thriving on controversy, the editor delivered himself of freewheeling personal opinions. He had no libel laws to worry about, but he often suffered some concern for his personal safety at the hands of citizens who objected to his opinions. One offending editor was tarred and feathered; others were pummelled, bullwhipped, knifed, and challenged to duels. More usual were shouting matches along the boardwalk or in the saloon—two of a reporter's main working arenas. Thus, a leather-lunged editor could become as much participant as observer in the madcap events he covered.

The raw individualism of the frontier was mirrored in the very titles of its newspapers. Nevada's two earliest were the *Gold Canyon Switch* and the *Genoa Scorpion.* Later appeared Virginia City's *Daily Trespass,* Battle Mountain's *Measure for Measure,* and the *Waubuska Mangler,* though this one later turned out to be a hoax. The town of Potosi, Nevada, had two rival sheets: *East of the Nevada; or the Miner's Voice from the Colorado,* and the eccentric *Potosi Nix Cum Rouscht.* Eastern California's best-known mining camp paper was the *Death Valley Chuck Walla.* From Utah came such journals as the *Censor,* the *Rustler,* the *Women's Exponent,* and *Kirk Anderson's Valley Tan.*

But it was Virginia City's *Territorial Enterprise* that stood head and shoulders above the rest. Here gathered a whole array of unusual talent—including a down-at-the-heels prospector who signed his columns "Mark Twain."

Small or large, defunct or successful, these early journals handed down to us the facts, feelings, and spirit of a unique era.

METEORIC rise and fall of mining camps was set down in many of their one-room newspaper offices. This one was located in eastern Nevada's White Pine County, now the locale of a number of ghost towns.

Mining Camp Finance: THE WHEELER-DEALERS' HEYDAY

The frenetic Comstock rush of 1860 attracted more than prospectors and job-seekers: it also brought out the speculators. As one incredibly rich strike followed another, an outdoor stock market blossomed along Virginia's muddy streets. And before long, the huge volume and variety of Comstock shares traded in San Francisco became the backbone of that city's new Stock Exchange.

But communications between market and mine were poor, and in the almost total absence of controls, dangerous and dishonest financial practices became rampant. Price quotations fluctuated wildly: early in 1875, the total value of all Comstock shares more than tripled in six weeks. When the market plummeted two years later, twenty thousand San Franciscans were reduced to living on charity.

Out of all this emerged a generation of financial tycoons: William C. Ralston, William Sharon, John W. Mackay, James G. Fair, James C. Flood, and others. With the untrammeled egoism of classic capitalists, they founded banks, donated to charities, and built such lavish residences as the Mackay mansion, which remains one of Virginia City's highlights.

By 1880, the Comstock was waning—attraction had shifted to other areas of Nevada and eastern California. But not until after the turn of the century did the promise of a large-scale bonanza appear southeast of Carson City. There, in the treeless desert, appeared three very promising new sites: Tonopah, Goldfield, and Rhyo-lite. At first, no one seemed willing to gamble hard cash on any of them—memories of financial shenanigans on the Comstock were too fresh.

Then the investors changed their minds, and from 1903 to 1907 there was a wild orgy of speculation in southeastern Nevada mining shares. Tonopah opened a stock exchange in 1902, Goldfield in 1905, Rhyolite in 1907. The paper boom was fueled not only by the true richness of the ores and full utilization of new communications media such as the telegraph, but by shady methods of capitalization designed to tempt the unwary—and, even more, by intensive public relations work. Every old trick and a number of new ones were used to swell investment at a feverish rate. Promoters bought enough ad space in national papers to get their accompanying "news dispatches" printed verbatim. They bribed editors and publishers with stock, staged publicity stunts such as world's championship prize fights and excursion trains, and combined stock touting with land promotion. The money poured in—especially from the East.

Inevitably, the bubble burst. A nationwide depression in 1907 put good companies and bad out of business, reminding many of Mark Twain's advice to an earlier generation: "There are two times in a man's life when he should not speculate; when he can't afford it and when he can." In the pangs of this relearned lesson were born a number of Nevada's most authentic ghost towns.

PAPER GOLD flooded the market to back every conceivable kind of Nevada mining enterprise. Naive investors poured their hard-earned cash into the pockets of the wheeler-dealers.

SPANKING NEW *stock exchange opened at Tonopah, Nevada, on December 31, 1902. Only two daily sessions were held—at eleven in the morning and at two-fifteen in the afternoon—but the turnover volume was huge, the atmosphere tense and frenzied.*

GOLDFIELD, NEVADA
"I LAY CLAIM...ONE THOUSAND FEET UP IN THE AIR"

Though the center of some of the most outrageous stock promotion in American history, Goldfield was solidly based in some very valuable ore deposits. One modest-sized mine alone chalked up five million dollars' income in a hundred and six days. As thousands flocked to this barren, volcanic land in 1903, the race for lots and claims became so frantic that one exasperated late-comer scrawled on a survey board: "I lay claim from this point one thousand feet up in the air. Now beat that you damn land sharks."

A jolly practice called "highgrading" became widespread: a mine employee's wages were negligible compared to the value of the nuggets he managed to stash in his underwear at the end of the day. One mine owner recalled, "Business was so good that the first manager we hired stole ten thousand dollars in the first month without our even suspecting it." The atmosphere in bar, brothel, and gambling den was summed up by one Goldfielder's comment that "You couldn't hardly notice the difference between three o'clock in the afternoon and three o'clock the next morning."

From a ramshackle camp, Goldfield swelled into a major town. In 1910, while the mines poured out over eleven million dollars, the population hit twenty thousand. But there were many problems. Food and water were scarce in this wasted desert where, as one housewife lamented, "a fresh blade of grass would bring you down on your knees to worship." Poor sanitation contributed to outbreaks of pneumonia and smallpox. But improved transportation—especially the railroad—ameliorated many of the hardships, and flush Goldfield even became a center of auto racing.

Yet the end was near. When the gold dwindled, people left in droves; most of them had gone by 1920. Torn by a series of fires and floods, Goldfield became a virtual ghost, its few residents huddling among reminders of past glories.

From Tonopah, go twenty-six miles south on U.S. 95 to Goldfield. Or from Las Vegas go one hundred eighty-one miles northwest to the town. Tonopah contains many abandoned mines; nearest true ghosts are Belmont and Ione, to the north; Candelaria, to the northeast; and Gold Point, to the south.

a GHOST TOWN worth seeing

ONCE-PROUD Goldfield Hotel cost half a million dollars to build in 1910. It was launched with a party lasting three days, during which the champagne ruined most of the fancy leather furniture and was even said to have flowed out the front door and down the street. Today its elegant appointments are in tatters.

PILLARED PORCH, its decadence worthy of the Old South, stands among many such victims of a half-century of neglect in Goldfield's residential section.

UNBOUNDED PROSPERITY *ruled Goldfield, Nevada, and the town took eagerly to such luxuries as the horseless carriage. The first one lurched into town on August 10, 1904—but couldn't be started again for the trip back to Tonopah.*

FORLORN under the stars, the shell of one of Rhyolite's four great bank buildings looks almost like a classical ruin. Situated at the end of the Amargosa desert, not far from Death Valley, the Nevada ghost town enjoyed a mining boom from 1905 to 1910.

GOLD POINT, Nevada, offers a smattering of desert buildings, an old mine complex, a few occupied trailers, a quaint post office clinging to life by a thread, and, a little distance away, this group of deserted false-front stores.

Loneliest Haunts: GHOSTS OF THE CALIFORNIA-NEVADA BORDER

This forgotten and desolate land harbors some of the truest of the true ghost towns. Here the air is sparkling clear, the sky a perfect bowl, the silence absolute. Is it any wonder the desert breeds myths?

LIKE SOME HOLLOW-EYED DESERT BEAST, a ruined store gazes out at those who pass the scanty remains of Leadfield, California, on the one-way road which leads down into Death Valley's spectacular Titus Canyon.

Fire! THE TOWN'S WORST ENEMY

In the headlong rush to build a camp, no thought was given to potential civic problems. It was every man for himself, because nobody knew how long the boom would last. While everybody wanted expensive luxuries as soon as possible, no one wanted to think about building codes, sewers, water systems, or fire departments. Until disaster struck.

Crowded together along narrow streets, the false-fronted buildings were perfect firetraps. Mining explosives were stored wherever space could be found. All through the Great Basin the situation was worsened by the dry, windy climate and lack of water. Once started, a fire could quickly devastate a town. Many camps burned again and again before effective countermeasures were devised.

A fire at Virginia City in 1875 burned two thousand buildings, with damage estimated at over ten million dollars. As described by one horror-struck onlooker: "firemen had abandoned all hopes of staying it by the ordinary methods. No rain had fallen for six months, everything was like tinder. . . . The streets were filled with flying people, furniture brought out of the houses was burning on the sidewalk . . . loose horses from the stables were dashing madly to and fro seeking to escape, with the hair all burned from their backs. . . . The flames came tearing on with a front 200 yds. wide and 200 ft. high." Even more horrible were fires in the mines themselves, which the men feared more than a cave-in: "Let but a splinter of pine be held in a candle . . . and there is a commotion such as is seen when a hive of bees is disturbed."

Efficient or not, the fire brigade was often a mining camp's earliest symbol of civic pride. Whenever a traveling photographer came through, the firemen trotted out to pose in full regalia. Their colorful old equipment is still on view in many ghost towns. Virginia City's fire companies were special: they became exclusive clubs, vying with each other less for fire-fighting accomplishments than for athletic prowess and social prestige. It was out of both pride and practicality that the mining frontier conferred a special status on its firemen.

MANY HATS of William Pennison, for sixteen years chief engineer of Virginia City's professional fire brigade, included memberships in the Odd Fellows, Mechanics' Union, and Exempt Firemen's Association. Mining camp firemen were club conscious and often enjoyed high social status.

DISASTROUS FIRES hit Tonopah, Nevada (upper right), and Goldfield (right). When fire struck a mining camp, the whole town was sometimes wiped out. If the mines were still booming, the town would rebuild before the embers cooled. But fire could suddenly turn an already declining camp into a ghost town.

BODIE, CALIFORNIA
"GOODBYE, GOD, I'M GOING TO BODIE."

a GHOST TOWN worth seeing

From Carson City, Nevada, head south for eighty-two miles on U.S. 395 to Bridgeport, California; continue seven miles farther, turn east on unpaved road which winds through barren hills for thirteen miles to reach Bodie.

Here is possibly the best all-round ghost town in the West. Far enough off the main road to discourage cursory vandals, it is protected as a State Park, though it doesn't have the orderly feel of one. Its dozens of deep-grained, russet-and-gold wooden buildings are discreetly maintained in a condition of "arrested decay" while the weeds grow freely around the many scattered artifacts.

Things were not so delicate in the old days. Bodie's sixty-five saloons were notorious. One preacher summed up the town as a "sea of sin, lashed by the tempests of lust and passion." In the poor cribs and elegant bagnios of Maiden Lane and Virgin Alley, such girls as Beautiful Doll, Madame Moustache, and Rosa May were sometimes rewarded with golden nuggets as tips. Violence was commonplace. "There is some irresistible power," commented the *Bodie Standard*, "that impels us to cut and shoot each other to pieces." Whether the notorious "bad man from Bodie" was actually a single person or a composite of Washoe Pete, Tom Adams, and Rough-and-Tumble Jack is still debated; the character became, in any case, a legend throughout the West. And the little girl whose family was moving from Aurora to Bodie, and who concluded her evening prayers with "Goodbye, God, I'm going to Bodie," was so widely quoted that one civic-minded newspaperman tried to claim she had really said, "Good, by God, I'm going to Bodie!"

Don't try to visit Bodie in the winter: the temperature drops to twenty or thirty below, with ten to twenty feet of snow. The venerable town is delightful, however, in spring and summer—as long as you remember to bring your lunch and don't mind the thirteen miles of washboard road going in.

"BAD, BAD BODIE" provided this little jail with plenty of customers. Murders allegedly occurred about once a day—at least until June of 1881, when the Bodie Daily Free Press reported that "Bodie is becoming a quiet summer resort—no one killed here last week."

GHOSTLY SPIRITS float undisturbed in the still air of Bodie's little Methodist Church, now that the classic structure has been closed to visitors. Vandals stole many of the interior ornaments, including an oilcloth imprinted with the Ten Commandments, one of which, of course, is "Thou Shalt Not Steal."

DAWN SHEDS a warm glow on Bodie's weathered storefronts, as it
has for more than a hundred summers. But in winter the snow often piles
as high as twenty feet, leaving only the tops of the buildings exposed
and bearing out the complaint of the early prospectors that Bodie had
''the worst climate out of doors.'' Since there are no tourist facilities,
visitors must rise very early to reach Bodie at dawn.

CLOSE LOOKING brings glimpses of early-day life in Bodie. Top left: Utilizing whatever materials were available, builders formed metal sidings from patterned Victorian sheet iron, flattened tin cans, and other oddments. Left: a bedstead in one of the frame houses on Bodie Bluff. Above: stout rigging of one of Bodie's all-important freight wagons.

ITS EDGES CURLED by time, this old boardwalk rises and falls along Main Street in front of the Miners' Union Hall, the Odd Fellows Hall, and the brick post office.

VENERABLE FAÇADE once welcomed Bodie's roistering Odd Fellows to their lodge. Built in 1878, the two-story hall also served as a meeting place for members of the Bodie Athletic Club.

Land Grab: BOOMVILLE HASTENS EASTWARD

When the first, wild initial Comstock excitement had begun to simmer down, prospectors grew restless. Spreading out into the virtually unexplored regions to the east, these ragged-looking fellows evolved into a class of shrewd, tough, professional ore seekers. Distinguishing themselves from mere miners, they were proud of their ability to survive in the harsh environment of central and eastern Nevada and western Utah.

But, as one authority noted, there were "a very large number of false starts for every one real success" in this area. In working a claim, prospectors and miners alike found that their greatest problem was the complex ores, which required smelting, and thus required more sophisticated knowledge and equipment than on the Comstock or in California. Three miles south of the ghost town of Ward, Nevada, for example, you can still see the huge, beehive-like ovens which supplied the Ward smelters (there are similar charcoal ovens in Death Valley: see pages 106-7). Timber remained a problem. In this largely treeless land, wood was so scarce that when one mining camp died, the lumber would often be carted off to the site of the next hoped-for bonanza.

"Greater than the Comstock!" was the usual—and always inaccurate—cry which would bring hundreds or even thousands flocking to some unheard-of point. Present-day Austin was the center of one important early boom, the 1862 Reese River rush; the town's many authentic, remaining buildings make it an important stop on any current itinerary of old Central Nevada mining camps. Eureka, about sixty miles farther east, has some interesting buildings dating from the 1870's and 1880's, when an impressive output of silver and lead made the Eureka mining district the second largest in Nevada.

But it was the sudden booms and busts in even more remote places—such as Belmont, Manhattan, Ione, Berlin, Grantsville, Rawhide, Fairview, and Wahmonie—that created Nevada's really classic ghost towns. All of these can still be seen, except for Fairview, which is within a naval bombing range, and Wahmonie, now part of a nuclear testing area.

Farther east, White Pine County experienced one of the most violent silver excitements ever known. Beginning in 1868, thousands of persons stampeded to White Pine; millions of dollars poured out. Two years later, it was all over, leaving only such desolate ghost towns as Treasure City, Hamilton, and Ward to bear witness. The semi-ghost of Pioche, farther south, is worth seeing for its long defunct "Million Dollar Courthouse."

In central and eastern Nevada, as in the Tonopah-Goldfield area, land booms were frequently tied in with the mining property and mining stock booms. And one ghost town—Tobar—was left in the wake of inflated agricultural land promotion: Tobar's boosters had falsely claimed that the desert sagebrush was about to be replaced by farms, ranches, and apple orchards. Another agricultural ghost, Grafton, slumbers at the edge of Utah's Zion National Park.

NEW INVENTION, the telegraph, quickly became a favorite tool of speculators in land, stocks, and mining claims.

PLACERVILLE AND ST. JOSEPH

Overland Telegraph Company.

— OFFICES AT —

PLACERVILLE, STRAWBERRY VALLEY, CHIPPIN'S STATION, FORT CHURCHILL,

GENOA, CARSON CITY, VIRGINIA CITY.

Connecting at Placerville with all the California Lines.

DISPATCHES FORWARDED TO ANY PART OF THE ATLANTIC STATES, BY "PONY EXPRESS."

All Messages Strictly Confidential.

Office Hours from 8, A. M. to 9, P. M. Sundays, 9 to 11, A. M. & 6 to 7 P. M.

San Francisco May 28 1861

To C. L. Strong

Selected site below town - See about title and arrange accordingly

John O. Earl

LATE TO BLOOM, quick to wither, was the town of Wahmonie, in Nevada's Nye County. This ghost may no longer be visited because it is in a nuclear testing range.

STAR-SPANGLED PROCESSION jolted down the dusty streets of Round Mountain to celebrate the Fourth of July, 1907. The town is one of the many ghosts of Nye County, in south-central Nevada.

a GHOST TOWN worth seeing

From Fallon, take U.S. 50 approximately thirty-five miles southeast to State 31; go twenty miles south to a locked gate marked "Scheelite", backtrack a few yards, and take dirt road heading southeast around the hills; take all righthand forks, about five miles to Rawhide.

HISTORY on the wall as insulation reveals that someone stayed here as late as the 1930's. Long after Rawhide died, individual miners showed up to take small amounts of "color" out of surrounding hills.

In 1907 a handful of men were working a mine at the edge of a wide, flat, barren valley. In 1909 they were still there, doing pretty much the same thing, and still earning a modest take.

Only—the intervening year had been a bit unusual. Eight thousand people had suddenly descended on the desert fastness. They feverishly built a modern town with all the latest features: telephones, a water system, a refrigeration plant—and one hundred twenty-five broker's offices. Then, in September, fire raged through the new town. As if by prearranged signal, the people deserted by the thousands.

Why had they come in the first place? They came on faith—on hope. Rawhide seemed like the last great chance to get in on the ground floor of a mining bonanza. A nationwide depression had thrown many of them out of work, and boom times in Goldfield had been interrupted by labor strife.

But above all, the people were lured by fantastic newspaper and magazine publicity proclaiming the area's supposedly rich mining potential. The people didn't bother to read the mining press, which pooh-poohed the whole affair. Nor did they check up on the notorious promoters who planted the news items, peddled stock, and sold downtown lots for up to $20,000. Rawhide's nine banks were open until midnight, but her main industry was gambling.

Within months, the highly-touted mines turned out to be ninety-percent hot air. Land values plummeted, and the disillusioned multitudes left as quickly as they had come. The West's most incredible boom-and-bust was over.

Today Rawhide is a total ghost, with only a few teetering buildings and shacks still standing. The most substantial is the old stone jail, and inside it, two massive, iron-ribbed prisoners' cages.

BOOM YEAR of Rawhide
was 1908, although enough
buildings remained in this
1909 photo to give an idea
of the town's incredible size.

WONDER Lumber Co.'s
chief executive must not have
appreciated the irony of his
firm's name until the boom
collapsed. Or perhaps he
was a native of Wonder,
Nevada, soon to suffer the
same fate as Rawhide.

Dusty Desertions: GHOSTS OF CENTRAL NEVADA

Ribbed by treeless mountain chains and bleak valleys, central Nevada became the destination for restless prospectors seeking another Comstock Lode. Though they never found one, they did spark a series of lesser booms, leaving some tragi-comic treasures for today's ghost town buffs.

A HUNDRED HOUSES dotted Ione, Nevada, in 1864, but only a few remain. Even in Ione's heyday the mines had their ups and downs, and after 1880 there were hardly any more ups.

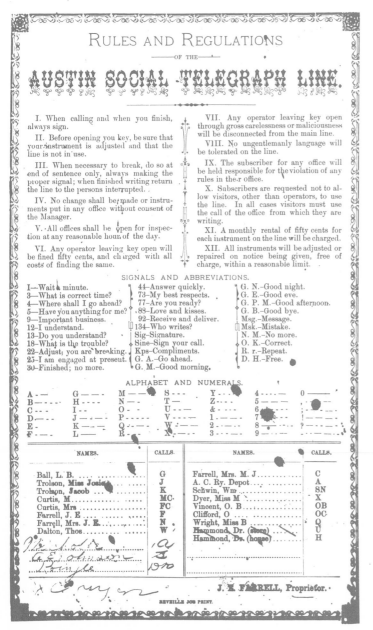

RULES AND REGULATIONS
— OF THE —
AUSTIN SOCIAL TELEGRAPH LINE.

I. When calling and when you finish, always sign.

II. Before opening you key, be sure that your instrument is adjusted and that the line is not in use.

III. When necessary to break, do so at end of sentence only, always making the proper signal; when finished writing return the line to the persons interrupted.

IV. No change shall be made or instruments put in any office without consent of the Manager.

V. All offices shall be open for inspection at any reasonable hour of the day.

VI. Any operator leaving key open will be fined fifty cents, and charged with all costs of finding the same.

VII. Any operator leaving key open through gross carelessness or maliciousness will be disconnected from the main line.

VIII. No ungentlemanly language will be tolerated on the line.

IX. The subscriber for any office will be held responsible for the violation of any rules in their office.

X. Subscribers are requested not to allow visitors, other than operators, to use the line. In all cases visitors must use the call of the office from which they are writing.

XI. A monthly rental of fifty cents for each instrument on the line will be charged.

XII. All instruments will be adjusted or repaired on notice being given, free of charge, within a reasonable limit.

SIGNALS AND ABBREVIATIONS.

1—Wait a minute.	44—Answer quickly.	G. N.—Good night.
3—What is correct time?	73—My best respects.	G. E.—Good eve.
4—Where shall I go ahead?	77—Are you ready?	G. P. M.—Good afternoon.
5—Have you anything for me?	88—Love and kisses.	G. B.—Good bye.
9—Important business.	92—Receive and deliver.	Msg.—Message.
12—I understand.	134—Who writes?	Msk.—Mistake.
13—Do you understand?	Sig—Signature.	N. M.—No more.
18—What is the trouble?	Sine—Sign your call.	O. K.—Correct.
22—Adjust; you are breaking.	Kps—Compliments.	R. r.—Repeat.
25—I am engaged at present.	G. A.—Go ahead.	D. H.—Free.
30—Finished; no more.	G. M.—Good morning.	

ALPHABET AND NUMERALS.

A .—	G —.	M ——	S ...	Y	4	0 —————
B —...	H	N —.	T —	Z	5 ———	
C .. .	I ..	O . .	U ..—	&	6	
D —..	J —.—.	P	V ...—	1 .——.	7 ——..	? —..—.
E .	K —.—	Q ..—.	W .——	2 ..—..	8 —....	
F .—.	L	R . ..	X .—..	3 ...—.	9 —..—	

NAMES.	CALLS.	NAMES.	CALLS.
Ball, L. B.	G	Farrell, Mrs. M. J	C
Trolson, Miss Josie	J	A. C. Ry. Depot	A
Trolson, Jacob	K	Schwin, Wm	SN
Curtis, M.	MC	Dyer, Miss M	X
Curtis, Mrs	FC	Vincent, O. B	OB
Farrell, J. E	F	Clifford, O	OC
Farrell, Mrs. J. E.	N	Wright, Miss B	Q
Dalton, Thos.	W	Hammond, Dr. (store)	U
		Hammond, Dr. (house)	H

J. X. FARRELL, Proprietor.

REVEILLE JOB PRINT.

NERVE CENTER of central and eastern Nevada's far-flung mining excitements in the 1860's, Austin gained that most lofty of distinctions: getting on the new-fangled telegraph line.

PRESIDING over Manhattan, Nevada, is this perky but empty little Catholic Church, which was moved over from nearby Belmont. Manhattan boomed in the early years of this century, then clung to life until 1946 on the payrolls of a three-thousand-ton gold dredge. But when the dredge was taken away, the town's residents followed, leaving Manhattan a virtual ghost.

Let 'em Roll! THE FRONTIER ON WHEELS

Ceaseless movement characterized the mining
excitements. Day and night the camps' rutted streets
were crowded with shouting skinners and their
groaning teams, fancy ladies in rollicking stages, and
buckboards clattering out to meet them.
Before long, these streets would know
a hundred years of silence.

THUNDERING DOWN the main street of Bodie, California, a ten-horse team hauls two wagonloads of what appears to be gunny sacks stuffed with provisions. Such freight meant life or death to the isolated settlements of the Great Basin.

FIVE WAGONS OF THE FRONTIER

CONESTOGA WAGONS, pulled by a team of
six horses, carried enormous freight cargos.
By the 1860's, the Conestoga had evolved
into the covered wagon, which had to be both
strong and light because the westering
pioneers often lowered them down ravines on
ropes. Top buggies, the sportscars of the
frontier, were invaluable if you were
a-courtin'. Concord coaches became the stage
coaches which carried up to 800 pounds of
cargo, plus passengers and precious bullion.
Buckboards had a variety of uses; some
individual pioneers who wished to travel
light and fast came West in them.

CONESTOGA

COVERED WAGON

SENIOR CITIZEN of Ione, Nevada, is this old utility wagon, which is slowly being engulfed by sagebrush.

TOP BUGGY

CONCORD COACH

BUCKBOARD

BELMONT, NEVADA
WIDE OPEN FOR NO BUSINESS

a GHOST TOWN worth seeing

From Tonopah, go east five miles on U.S. 6; take State 8A thirty-five miles north to State 69; turn east, continuing through Manhattan, and bearing northeast on unpaved road fourteen miles farther to Belmont.

Approaching Belmont from the south or east, you gaze across miles of desolate valley floor toward one of two tall chimneys which, like sentinels, guard the approaches to town. Built of brick molded and fired on the site, they reflect Belmont's rare fortune in having had a good natural supply of building materials—clay, rock, and wood.

Pleasantly tucked amid gentle hills, this is one of Nevada's best ghost towns, with many long-deserted stone, brick, and frame buildings. Grandest relic is the former Nye County Courthouse, a two-story brick edifice surmounted by a square cupola. Venturing inside, you pick your way across broken strips of lath and dusty shards of plaster, and, at your own risk, try the creaky staircase and even creakier steps leading up into the cupola. Don't miss the ruined jail, attached to the rear of the building.

In a century-old stone house on the main street lives Mrs. Rose Walter, Belmont's most venerable resident. After introducing you to her various pets, she'll point out the house where she was born and tell of growing up here—and of the town's great days before her birth, when the immense, forty-stamp Combination Mill was hauled over from Cisco, California, to pulverize some of the $15 million worth of silver and lead ores dug out before 1887. Belmont's twenty-year heyday came after the Comstock's, and was followed by the turn-of-the-century Tonopah boom which largely drained Belmont of its residents.

"THE COSMOPOLITAN" was many things to many people in its colorful career. In the 1870's the local paper announced that "chaste" plays were enacted "that can be witnessed by the most fastidious and squeamish."

BACK LANES of Belmont hold many rustic touches. A babbling stream, lined with cottonwoods, divides the town from its courthouse. Beyond the fence shown here are the backs of the main street buildings.

TALL CHIMNEY east of town is thought to have been part of the clay firing works which turned out the bricks used in building several of Belmont's larger structures.

BIGGEST AND BOLDEST ruin at Belmont is the gaunt brick skeleton of the old Highbridge ore mill. It is located off the main road, several hundred yards south of the round chimney.

GRAFTON, UTAH
DIXIE COTTON, ZION SILK

While most Great Basin ghost towns lie in bleak desert settings, Grafton is an exception. Amid orchards, mulberry trees, and lowing cows, the abandoned settlement slumbers beside the Virgin River, under the shadow of the dramatic cliffs of Zion National Park.

Grafton was founded about 1859 by five Mormon families. They had come with others to settle southern Utah, which they called "Dixie" because Brigham Young had decreed that the staple crop was to be cotton. Assisted by the friendly Paiute Indians, the families dammed the river for irrigation.

In 1862, disaster struck: A flood inundated the entire valley. As reported in Salt Lake City's *Deseret News*, "the houses in old Grafton came floating down with the furniture, clothing, and other property of the inhabitants . . . including three barrels of molasses." Realizing that floods were a special hazard in the area, the survivors moved their settlement to safer ground and dug a system of canals and ditches. Along with cotton, they planted corn, wheat, and tobacco. By 1865 they had two hundred acres under cultivation. In time, the raising of livestock also became important.

Tragedy struck again when the Indians went on the warpath. One settler after another was killed by marauding Paiutes—as Grafton's gravestones still testify. The men were forced to work their fields in armed groups; periodically, the whole town had to be evacuated. When, in the 1870's, the Indian threat abated, the settlers obtained Brigham Young's permission to plant mulberry trees and grow silkworms. Now the wives had comfortable, pretty silk dresses!

Although Grafton wilted toward ghost town status after 1907, its charm and spectacular setting were not lost on Hollywood: since 1950, portions of several films, including *Butch Cassidy*, have been shot here.

a GHOST TOWN worth seeing

From St. George, west of Zion National Park go nine miles northeast on Interstate 15; then take State 15 twenty-seven miles east to Rockville. Here, get local directions for unpaved road which leads southwest about two miles to Grafton.

VICTIMS OF INDIAN ATTACKS, and other Grafton settlers, are buried in this well-kept Mormon cemetery which lies on the road southeast of town.

SPECTACULAR SETTING, under the cliffs of Zion National Park, makes Grafton one of the West's most photogenic ghost towns. The reddish earthen building was a Mormon meeting center and school.

GHOST TOWNS OF WESTERN NEVADA (*Gold Hill,* on State 79 south of Virginia City; *Genoa,* on State 57, east off U.S. 395 about 10 mi. south of Carson City; *Dayton,* east of Carson on U.S. 50; *Sutro,* 1 mi. north of U.S. 50, from point 7 mi. east of Dayton; *Fort Churchill,* northeast of Dayton, east off U.S. 50 on State 2B; *Pine Grove,* southeast of Carson, south of U.S. 95 Alternate at Yerington on State 3, for 10 mi., then, southeast on gravel surface known as "Walker River Ranch" or "Pine Grove Flat" road about 10 mi., turn right at junction and keep right 5 mi.; *Aurora,* Walker River Ranch road as if for Pine Grove, or else State 3C 3 mi. north of it—about 48 mi. south of State 3 take left fork about 5 mi.; *Candeleria,* southeast of Hawthorne, 5 mi. west of U.S. 95 on dirt road from 12 mi. north of Coaldale; *Gold Point,* south of Tonapah, on State 71, 14 mi. southwest of U.S. 95 at Stonewall; and *Rhyolite,* between Tonopah and Las Vegas, west of U.S. 95 on State 58 and State 90). This is the richest strip of ghost towns in the Great Basin. They can be visited conveniently along with Bodie, Virginia City, Goldfield, and the ghost towns of east-central California. Genoa, the oldest town in Nevada, is a partial ghost, tastefully restored and in a beautiful setting. Dayton is a semi-ghost with many old storefronts. Sutro, privately owned, is sometimes open to the public and sometimes not; its main point of interest is the boarded-up mouth of the Sutro Tunnel. Fort Churchill (see photo), a State Historic Monument, was Nevada's first and largest military outpost. The others are pure ghosts, mostly for dyed-in-the-dust buffs only. However, Rhyolite's gaunt skeletons, bottle house, and picturesque railway depot are equally fascinating to both enthusiast and casual tourist. Barren desert country, except in the case of Genoa.

GHOST TOWNS OF NORTHERN NEVADA (*Jarbidge,* north of Elko, 52 mi. on State 51 to gravel road leading east 20 mi., then north 26 mi. on precipitous hairpin road; *Tuscarora,* northwest of Elko, 24 mi. on State 51 to State 11, northwest 20 mi. to gravel State 18, west 7 mi.; *Galena,* southeast of Winnemucca, south of U.S. 80 on State 8A about 13 mi., dirt road west about 2 mi.; *Unionville,* southwest of Winnemucca 29 mi. on U.S. 80 to State 50, south 16 mi., west 4 mi. on dirt spur; *Lower Rochester,* continue past the Unionville road to just beyond "new" Rochester). These are all relatively minor ghost towns, for purists. Inquire at Jarbidge for location of the old mill. Tuscarora may be approached from the west via the secondary ghosts of Golconda and Midas. Galena (see photo) is a rich area for rockhounds. Unionville, now in ruins, was once a substantial city. Desert plateaus, except for mountainous Jarbidge.

The Great Basin

GHOST TOWNS OF EASTERN CALIFORNIA
(*Cerro Gordo*, west of Death Valley, east of
U.S. 395 on State 136, then east 6 mi. on
steep switchback gravel road; *Ballarat*, west
of Death Valley, 31 mi. north of Trona, then
about 5 mi. east on dirt road; *Panamint City*,
from Ballarat go north about 2½ mi., then
east on dirt road into Surprise Canyon, last
few miles by foot; *Skidoo*, in Death Valley,
about 10 mi. south of State 190 at Ranger
Station, 8 mi. northeast on dirt road; and
Death Valley Charcoal Kilns, on Panamint
Highway, then about 9 mi. east of
Wildrose Ranger Station). Pure ghosts, of
which Cerro Gordo is the most extensive.
The enormous charcoal kilns are fascinating
remnants of mining days in this area where
wood was precious. There's little left of
Skidoo (see photo) except for the old mining
buildings located on precipitous roads above
the townsite. This barren, hilly region is
too hot and dry to visit in summer.

GHOST TOWNS OF CENTRAL NEVADA (*Austin*, about 130 mi. east of
Reno on U.S. 50; *Ione* and *Berlin*, southeast of Fallon, south of U.S. 50 on
State 23 to junction 1 mi. north of Gabbs, then east on State 91 and
State 21; *Manhattan*, about 75 mi. south of Austin, then 7 mi. east on
State 69). Austin (see photo) is still a living town with many quaint,
empty buildings as evidence of a more glorious past. Ione and Berlin, both
near Ichthyosaur Paleontologic State Monument, are lonely ghosts with
modest wooden structures; Berlin's huge, ruined ore mill is fun to explore.
Manhattan is a near-ghost whose classic little church was moved over from
Belmont (see page 102). Gas is *usually* available at Ione, but in this area
it's wise to fill up before leaving the main roads. Arid, sparsely populated
desert hills and valleys.

GHOST TOWNS OF WESTERN UTAH (*Silver Reef*, west of Zion
Canyon, northeast of St. George about 15 mi. to Leeds, west
1 mi. on dirt road; *Ophir*, west of Provo across Utah Lake, from
U.S. 15, west on State 73 about 35 mi. to junction with gravel
road, then east 4 mi.). Silver Reef, not far from Grafton (see
page 105), consists mainly of the Wells Fargo Office and a
scattering of stone foundations and ruins. The beautiful Mormon
church (see photo) in the little town of Pine Valley, northwest of
Silver Reef, is well worth seeing. Ophir contains a number of empty
houses and other small wooden buildings, but is partially occupied.
Its neighbor to the southeast, Mercur, is sometimes billed as a
ghost town but is now virtually demolished. Except for lush
Pine Valley, bleak desert settings, although, geographically, all
except Mercur and Ophir lie in the Colorado Plateau.

HUSTLE AND BUSTLE of the mining frontier was nowhere more evident than in Cripple Creek, Colorado, during the 1890's. After producing nearly half a billion dollars worth of gold, Cripple Creek collapsed and became a near ghost. The old-time town has recently reawakened as a tourist center.

ROCKY MOUNTAIN
SPREADING FEVER
1859...

NOW IT WAS COLORADO'S TURN. The tale first told in California's Sierra foothills and already unfolding in Nevada's Comstock was about to be told again—with exaggerations. GOLD IN KANSAS TERRITORY!! were the words flashed across the nation in the first newspaper dispatches of a bonanza in the Colorado mountains. Fleeing the after-effects of the depression of 1857, a new generation of gold-seekers adopted the motto *Pike's Peak or Bust!* and became known as "59'ers."

But the ups and downs of gold rush life soon proved even more frustrating in the Rockies than in the Far West. Instant towns went up—and became instant ghost towns. Of the hundred thousand hopefuls who, according to one authority, started across the plains in 1859, only half even reached the rallying point called Denver; and half of these promptly turned around and went home. "Humbug of humbugs," they called Colorado.

Yet those who stayed helped to roll back an important new frontier. Hope returned as experienced, professional miners began arriving from California and elsewhere. New discoveries laid the basis for substantial towns all the way from southern Colorado to northern Idaho, and from western Montana down to eastern Utah—a vast territory which had hitherto been only a wilderness. But even the larger communities were not immune from the gyrations of fortune. Life on the mountainous frontier was still hard and uncertain— as late as the 1870's only one child out of two lived to its third birthday—and there were many ghost towns still in the making.

The camps' life cycles were remarkably similar. The early, flush days were exciting and full of optimism. Suddenly the easily-worked surface gold gave out; gloom settled over the camp, and its population dwindled. Then the late 1860's and early 1870's brought dramatic breakthroughs in transportation and technology. The town woke up as the railroad came whistling in, bringing along vital supplies and hauling away heavy ores. Big new machines hammered away at the tough rocks, and, following on the Comstock example, the treasure seekers focused not only on gold but on glittering silver. While the saloons again ran at full tilt, refinement also came to the frontier. A Montana debating society even posed the question: "Resolved, that the Love of Woman has had more influence upon the Mind of Man than the Love of Gold." Yet in time the hard-rock deposits, too, began to give out. A final blow was the collapse of the silver market in 1893, brought on by demonitization.

Strewn in the wake of this wide arc of boom and bust, the Rocky Mountain ghost towns are today among the richest and wryest of their kind. The old wooden structures lean more precariously each year, under the twin pressures of winter snows and vandalism. Occasional brick and stone buildings, more resistant to fire and the elements, remind us of the Victorian era's sense of civic pride. And some larger towns—like Central City, Colorado—have lately been rescued from ghostly limbo to become tourist centers, with good displays of treasured artifacts and old photographs.

The adventurous will welcome Colorado's justly famous high-altitude jeep trails, rugged routes which twist through some of America's most spectacular scenery on the way to the more isolated ghost towns. The jolting ride's the thing in most cases, though, because few of the remote towns can match the more accessible ones in style and number of surviving structures. Eastern Utah and northern Idaho are slimmer pickings (southern Idaho is covered in Chapter Four). But western Montana holds some special treats for ghost towners.

Most of the best Rocky Mountain ghosts and semi-ghosts can be reached easily by passenger car in summer. Winter trips may take more nerve, but often reward the visitor with an incomparable mood of snowy stillness.

THE ROCKIES AND THEIR GHOST TOWNS

✗ True Ghost Town: Majority of buildings disused; few if any residents; no modern facilities.

✹ Partial Ghost Town: Some disused buildings; some residents; limited facilities.

★ Tourist Ghost Town: Old structures refurbished to promote old-time atmosphere; modern facilities.

🛡40 Interstate Highways

🛡80 U.S. Highways

🛡95 State Highways & Secondary Roads

NOTE: Map is as accurate as present information permits. Refer to detailed maps for minor roads, and always inquire locally about road conditions.

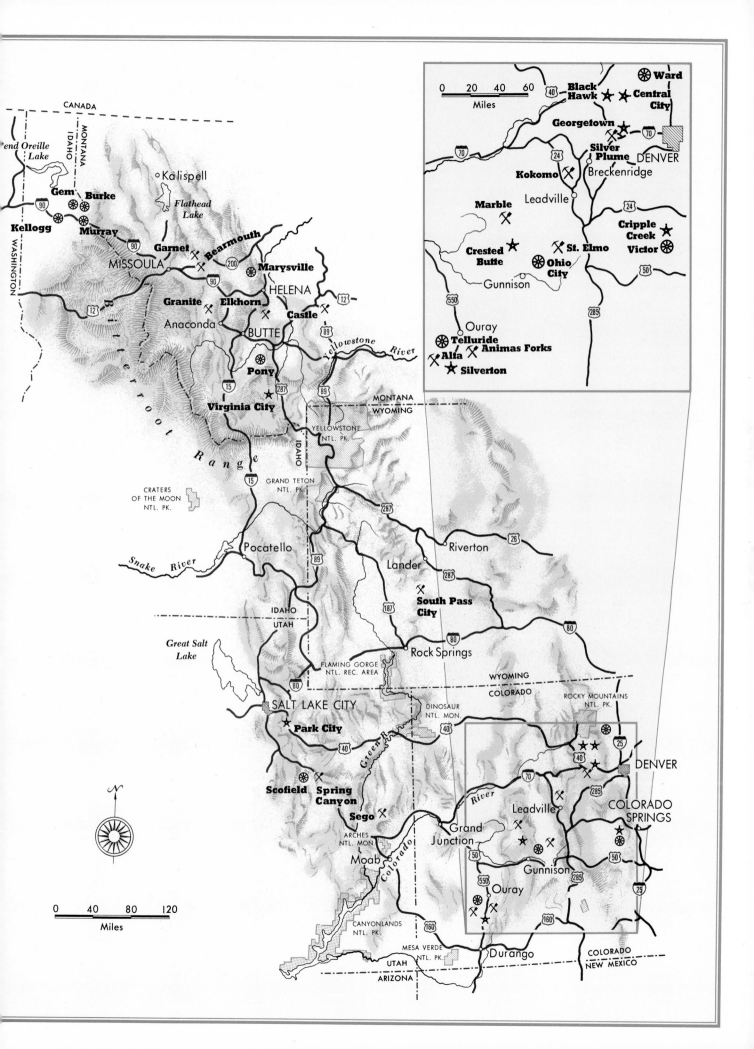

CANADA

end Oreille
Lake

MONTANA
IDAHO

○ Kalispell

Flathead
Lake

Gem ✹ **Burke**

90

Kellogg

WASHINGTON

Murray

Garnet ✕ **Bearmouth**

MISSOULA

200

Marysville ✹

90

HELENA

12

Granite **Elkhorn**

Anaconda

12

Castle ✕

BUTTE

89

Pony ✹

15

Yellowstone River

287

Virginia City ★

MONTANA
WYOMING

YELLOWSTONE
NTL. PK.

IDAHO

15

GRAND TETON
NTL. PK.

CRATERS
OF THE MOON
NTL. PK.

Snake River

Pocatello

89

287

187

26

Riverton

Lander

287

South Pass
City ✕

IDAHO
UTAH

Great Salt
Lake

80

Rock Springs

FLAMING GORGE
NTL. REC. AREA

WYOMING
COLORADO

80

ROCKY MOUNTAINS
NTL. PK.

SALT LAKE CITY

DINOSAUR
NTL. MON.

Green R.

Park City ★

40

40

DENVER

25

70

40

N

Scofield ✹ ✕ **Spring**
Canyon

Leadville

285

COLORADO
SPRINGS

Sego ✕

River

50

ARCHES
NTL. MON.

Grand
Junction

★

✹ ✕

285

50

Moab

Colorado

Gunnison

25

550

Ouray

160

CANYONLANDS
NTL. PK.

0   40   80   120

Miles

160

MESA VERDE
NTL. PK.

Durango

COLORADO
NEW MEXICO

UTAH
ARIZONA

Inset map:

0   20   40   60

Miles

40

✹ **Ward**

Black
Hawk ★ ★ **Central**
City

70

Georgetown ✕

24

70

Silver
Plume ✕

DENVER

Kokomo ✕

Breckenridge

Leadville

24

Marble ✕

Cripple
Creek ★

Crested ★
Butte

✕ **St. Elmo**

Victor ✹

Ohio ✹
City

Gunnison

50

550

285

Ouray

Telluride ✹

✕ **Animas Forks**

Alta ✕

Silverton ★

FIRST COMMERCIAL
establishment in a mining camp
was often a combination
restaurant, store, and saloon,
roofed with canvas stretched
over a log frame.

MINER'S MANNERS
were not dictated by
Emily Post, and their diet
was a nutritionist's nightmare. Whereas California's
gold region had at least a
few nearby farms, the early
Rocky Mountain miners had
almost no fresh food.

In the Rockies, as in California and Nevada, the early mining camps sprang up almost overnight, as people flocked in at the news of the earliest discoveries. Where the trapper and pioneer farmer had sought isolation and self-sufficiency, the miner obtained cash and wanted to spend it fast. Irreligious and footloose, he seldom arrived with a family, but craved the noise and ready companionship that only a town could provide. Very quickly, newly arrived merchants would be ready to accommodate him with goods and services previously unknown on the frontier.

The early miner lived in a tent or rude shack near his "diggins," and he often continued to live apart from the town. One diarist reported that "The people were camped all around . . . in wagons, tents and temporary brush houses or wickiups. The principal business houses were saloons, gambling houses, and dance halls, two or three so-called stores with very small stocks of general merchandise and little provisions." Besides saloonkeepers, merchants, and prostitutes, early arrivals included speculators, lawyers, salesmen, and the all-important freighters.

Speed was everything. No one knew how long the gravels would pay. But while they did, the merchant whose stock arrived first stood to profit as handsomely as the man who first found the gold, or the promoter who made the first subdivisions. In such an atmosphere, prices skyrocketed, then fluctuated wildly.

VICTORIAN PIN-UPS, cards, and months-old magazines were among a mining camp's few amusements—until the hurdy-gurdy girls made their appearance.

"MEN ARE FOOLS and women devils in disguise," observed Leadville's newspaper. "That's the reason the dance halls clear from one to two hundred dollars per night."

MRS. GRAMES' BOARDING
HOUSE was operated for miners
at Silver Reef, Utah, now a ghost
town. Residents much appreciated
a woman's touch in the cooking
and general atmosphere.

A MAN WHO COULD
COOK and was willing to
stay home from "prospects"
in the hills could earn high wages
in a boarding house kitchen.

Boarding Houses: FIRST COMFORTS OF CAMP LIFE

ONLY BEARS live now in this old boarding house in the ghost town of Alta, Colorado.

Some of the most prominent buildings still to be seen in the Rocky Mountain ghost towns are the old boarding houses and their cousins, the bunkhouses and boarding hotels.

Although the earliest miners camped and cooked for themselves, many of those who followed preferred to buy their food and lodging. While demand still far outstripped available buildings, partitioned tents served as sleeping rooms. As the town developed, the boarding house became one of its key institutions, offering respectable women jobs long before schools or laundries did. Accommodations were often quite rough, with floor space itself sometimes selling at premium prices. Travelers commented on the widespread sport of eavesdropping through the thin partitions.

The boarding houses kept improving along with the towns. Their popularity did not diminish with the introduction of a more diversified economy, industrialized mining methods, and the wage system. Eventually some mining companies began building bunkhouses and boarding houses for their men—prelude to the full-fledged "company towns" which were to emerge after the turn of the century.

Stoutly built, many ghost boarding houses have weathered the severe winters better than their neighbors. Exploring them today, one can only speculate on the identity of those who lived — and sometimes died—in their long-vacant rooms.

GARNET, MONTANA
STARTED LIFE EARLY—AND LOOKS IT

a GHOST TOWN worth seeing From Missoula, go approximately thirty-two miles southeast on Interstate 90 to Bearmouth. Take extremely steep, unpaved mountain road for approximately ten miles north to Garnet.

Anyone taking the incredibly steep, unpaved road up to Garnet today cannot fail to wonder at the stamina of the men who overcame such imposing barriers in order to mine the Rockies.

The Garnet winters were fierce. Many miners left for the season, but a few stayed behind to repair their equipment and pile up paydirt that couldn't be washed until spring. The story goes that once, when Garnet was snowed in and supplies ran out, a man made it all the way through the maze of underground tunnels to the neighboring town of Bearmouth.

Gold was found here in the early 1860's. Unlike many of Montana's long-vanished early boomtowns, Garnet enjoyed a moderate, if fluctuating, prosperity well into the twentieth century. Very old and tottering, some of its buildings have no foundations or floors at all, but are simply boards stuck in the ground. Although severely vandalized in the 1960's, Garnet is still an outstanding example of a primitive Rocky Mountain ghost town.

In 1970, a group of idealistic students had taken up residence in two of its cabins. Calling themselves the "Garnet Preservation Society," their worthy aims were to prevent further vandalism and decay, and to make precise drawings of the quaint structures.

RICHLY FORESTED hillsides rising all around Garnet are worth exploring for isolated structures, the ore mill itself, and pieces of old mining machinery such as this.

SWISS-CHALET snow bonnets cap Garnet's teetering buildings in winter. But don't try your car on the treacherous Garnet road at this time of year; seek the advice of local experts.

PRECARIOUS TILT of some of the town's buildings makes you wonder how they stand at all. The false-front structure at left was the store of T. A. Davey, who auctioned off the last of its antique contents in 1948.

ROUGH-HEWN JUSTICE
in the early towns was typified
by this vigilante hanging at
Helena, Montana. To replace
such "law by Judge Lynch,"
frontier officials were sworn in
(far right). And by the 1890's,
when severe industrial labor strife
raked northern Idaho's Coeur
d'Alene district, a full courtroom
system was ready to handle the
cases, culminating in Harry
Orchard's famous defense by
attorney Clarence Darrow, standing in the lower photo.

Civic Order: THE HARD-WON STRUGGLE

Independent, hard-living, untidy, and young, the man of the mining frontier was reluctant to admit the need for social order.

But the need was soon overwhelming. The town streets became mud holes in winter and spring, dust traps in summer, and obstacle courses and garbage dumps the year round. Problems of water and sanitation were frightful, and fire was a constant threat, as it had been in California and Nevada. Lawlessness took varied and rampant forms—claim-jumping, horse-stealing, stagecoach robbery, petty theft, forgery, confidence games, drunken shootouts. Instant urbanization had produced some of the outer trappings of civilization without the necessary underpinnings.

Almost from the first, there had been democratic miners' meetings, convened to settle questions of claims and to work out simple mining codes; these would pave the way for more advanced forms of civic cooperation. In the meantime, however, the vigilante committees sprang up. Controversial at best, the vigilantes offered a needed solution to real and urgent problems during a period of transition. But as the 1860's advanced, they wore out their welcome in one community after the next through Colorado, Utah, Montana, and Idaho. The vigilantes tended to attract questionable leadership and to exhibit all the drawbacks of justice without appeal.

As the town grew older, so did its average resident—and so did that resident's vested interest in a more stable social order. Gradually, the frontier's instinctive democracy evolved into a more graded power structure, with greater diversification of roles. Voting qualifications were often imposed, and professional civil servants began to appear. But it was always easier to plan a government than to pay for it, and there were howls of protest whenever anybody suggested taxes. Often, the easy way out— and one which helped soothe Puritan consciences—was to tax most heavily the "disreputable" (and very profitable) sector: the saloons and bawdy houses. This, in itself, was a sign that the times were changing.

DRAMA OF LATE AFTERNOON SUN accentuates the weathered textures of Elkhorn's classic Fraternity Hall (center) and a hotel thought to have been called The Metropolitan (left). These, and literally scores of other old *structures, make* Elkhorn one of the finest of Western ghost towns.' (See cover and page 146.)

ELKHORN, MONTANA
WALTZERS AND WORSE

Dating from the second wave of Montana's gold and silver rushes, Elkhorn has survived as one of the most extensive ghost towns in the West. Its principal mine, the Elkhorn, opened around 1872 and has changed hands repeatedly. Booming in the 1880's and '90's before tapering off in this century, the Elkhorn reputedly produced some $14 million in silver during its long life.

Although a few cabins have been re-occupied, the town retains the air of an abandoned period-piece. Scores of empty log and frame structures, brown and weathered, nestle in a small valley ringed with evergreen hills. Most were family dwellings: Elkhorn's miners worked for wages and brought their families with them. Many were foreigners — Dutch, Germans, Scandinavians, Irish, French, and Cornish. A colony of 500 woodchoppers occupied one end of town; their labors were essential for fueling the mills and warming the homes throughout Montana's bitter-cold winters.

Two hotels still stand, but the most striking building is the Fraternity Hall, with its castellated cornices and its unique second-story outcropping. A grand variety of lodges and other groups celebrated here, sometimes even staging prizefights in the spacious interior. Once, during a dance, two men got into a fight over what kind of music the band should play. The square-dancer shot the waltzer dead—and was later hanged for it.

a GHOST TOWN worth seeing

From Helena, take Interstate 15 (U.S. 91) twenty-eight miles south to Boulder; there turn southeast on State 281 for four miles, then northeast on a good but unpaved road approximately twelve miles to Elkhorn.

TIGHTLY CHINKED with lime to insulate residents against the fierce Montana winters, the square-hewn logs of this rustic Elkhorn cabin typify the building style of the "Treasure State's" nineteenth century mining camps.

Commerce: GAUGE OF TOWN GROWTH

In the precipitous Rockies, commerce depended to a crucial degree on the fluctuating conditions of mineral yield and transport. At first, the prices of every commodity gyrated wildly with every local rumor of boom or bust. Then, as the mining era matured and the distribution of ores became better known, merchants could make more permanent plans.

The dreadful state of the early freight routes was gradually alleviated by the appearance of toll roads and toll crossings, whose operators had to maintain them with at least occasional reliability. The opening of the direct Missouri River line from the Midwest was an unquestionable benefit to Montana. But it was the railroad, developing rapidly after the Union Pacific reached Cheyenne, Wyoming, in 1867, that made the big difference. Denver, in particular, profited by a series of new rail links; and all through the Rockies the cost of goods, as well as of smelting and labor, dropped sharply.

Now, with inventories deepening and diversifying, and with more and more specialized tradesmen on hand, the Rockies could urbanize at an accelerated pace.

1882.

Coulson Line!

Will run several of the Fastes and Best Boats on the Missouri this season.

Leaving Bismarck and Benton twice a week. Rates for the East or West furnished on application.

STEAMBOATS vied for passengers and cargo between the Midwest and the gold fields of Montana and northern Idaho.

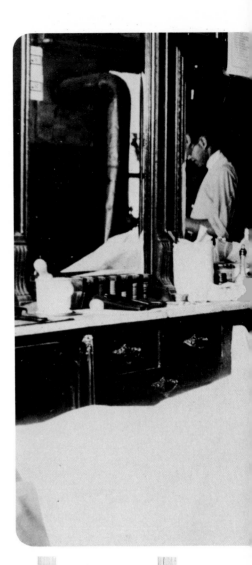

TOLL ROADS and toll crossings offered at least some incentive for keeping the vital freighting routes in good repair.

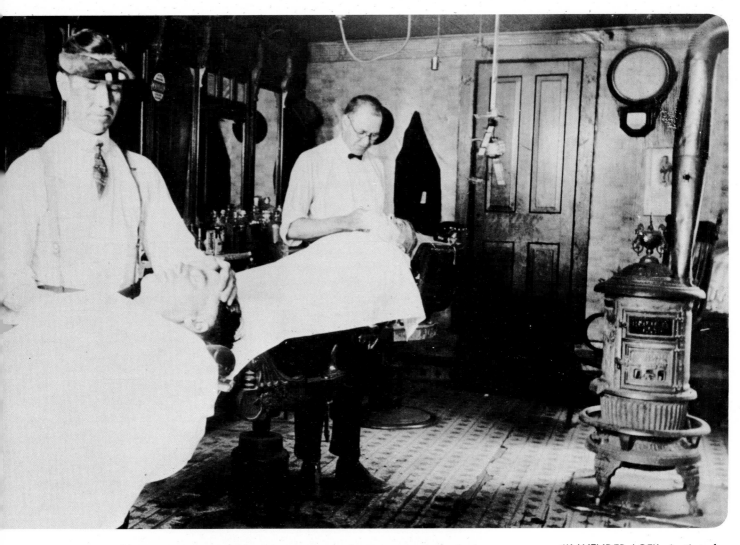

"LAVENDER AGE" niceties of a
shave and a haircut were readily
available in Park City's heyday,
but are harder to come by in
the half-deserted community
which has survived.

EXPANDING COMMERCE meant a well-heeled
gentleman could get a luxury hotel room
at Cripple Creek, Colorado. But when the
gold gave out, Cripple Creek withered.

TUGGED ALONG by a tiny donkey, visitors are conducted far back into the Bobtail Gold Mine, one of Colorado's deepest. It's located at the picturesque former mining camp of Black Hawk, a neighbor of Central City.

GETTING THE RICHES: THE STAMP MILL

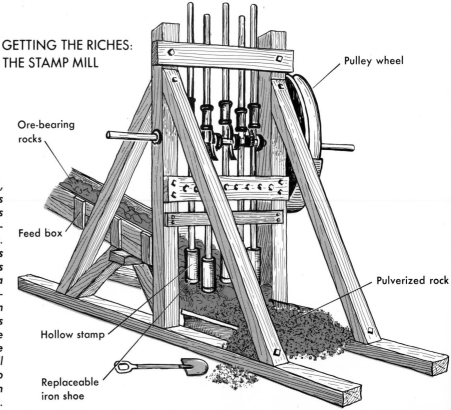

Pulley wheel

Ore-bearing rocks

Feed box

Pulverized rock

Hollow stamp

Replaceable iron shoe

SIMPLE BUT EFFECTIVE, stamp mills crushed the rocks under heavy iron pestles whose movement was controlled by a cam shaft. Though the noisy machines had been used for centuries in Europe, in 1851 California miners added the replaceable shoes, mounting them to rotate freely and thus wear out evenly—a feature which gained worldwide acceptance. Employed all through the West, stamp mills are today a common ghost town artifact.

Underground Era: RELIVING THE HARD-ROCK BOOM

Through most of the Rockies, the real treasure lay deep in the mountain rather than on the surface or in streams. Revisiting the old mines and machinery, one marvels at the pluck and ingenuity of the men who dug the tunnels, chipped away the tough rocks, and loaded them onto donkey-drawn carts to be hauled to the stamp mills.

IMMENSE, abandoned quarry above the ghost town of Marble, Colorado, shipped fine marble for public architecture all over the U.S., including a single piece worth over a million dollars for the Lincoln Memorial, and a fifty-five ton block for the Tomb of the Unknown Soldier.

REMARKABLE early photo, apparently made by magnesium flare, shows miners in underground workings at Elkhorn, Montana, which is now a ghost town (see page 121).

Old Mills: STOUTEST SURVIVORS OF THE MINING FRONTIER

The heart of a big-production mining camp was its mill complex, usually located near the outskirts of town. Less destructible than the town buildings, the hulking mills are today's best witness to the tough determination—and sizeable investment— that were needed to mine the Rockies.

CLOSED UP TIGHT, this old silver mill at Bay Horse, Idaho, is better preserved than most ghost mills. Like many, it was built on a hillside to take advantage of gravity in the flow of material.

MILLS VARIED widely according to local conditions, particularly the composition of the ores; yet many features were common. This idealized rendering is based on a type of Comstock silver mill influential in Rocky Mountain mill design. Though silver refining was usually more complex than gold, both metals often occurred in the same rocks and were treated similarly. Among the many pieces of equipment not shown here were concentrating tables, pulverizing mullers and dies, and amalgam retorts. Chemicals including mercury, were also added at various stages.

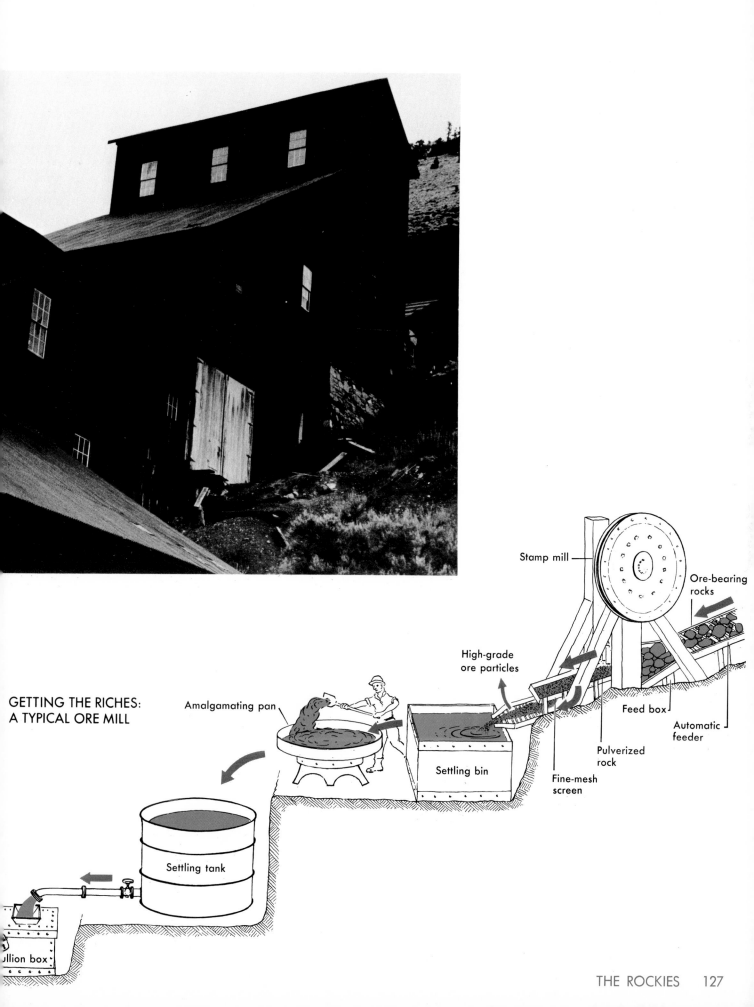

GETTING THE RICHES:
A TYPICAL ORE MILL

Stamp mill

Ore-bearing rocks

High-grade ore particles

Feed box

Automatic feeder

Pulverized rock

Fine-mesh screen

Amalgamating pan

Settling bin

Settling tank

llion box

CRAZY QUILT of light bars floods a silver mill at Elkhorn, Montana. Cows and horses have now adopted the structure as a kind of barn-away-from-home.

TIPPED AND STREWN
every which way are these ore carts, timbers, and other fragments of a once-rich gold mining complex at Ohio City, Colorado.

CASH FLOW no longer derives from this ore chute at Ohio City, Colorado (below, left); nor from the huge Silver King mill above Park City, Utah, now marked by acres of discarded cable and other supplies.

SILENT AND ALONE in winter, the Silver King mining complex at Park City, Utah, has seen far livelier days. It paid its owners over $5 million in profits.

SPRING CANYON/STANDARDVILLE, UTAH
BLEAK AND UNIQUE

a GHOST TOWN worth seeing

From Provo, go about sixty-nine miles southeast to Helper, on U.S. 50. Ask directions to Spring Canyon Road, and take this about four miles to Spring Canyon. Standardville is strung along the canyon farther up, with no visible demarcation between the two.

Butch Cassidy once slept here, but that's about all the Wild West history there is to Spring Canyon and its adjoining cousin, Standardville. For these unusual ghosts, both founded by Mormons, were twentieth-century company towns of Utah's coal-rich Carbon County, of the Colorado Plateau.

Like the ruins of an ancient city, the roofless walls of some sixty rock houses mark the site of the original town of Storrs, built for mine employees in 1912 and 1913. The name was changed to Spring Canyon in 1924. Nearby is the large school building and meeting house, still intact and partly used—and plastered with dire warnings to trespassers.

All along the right-hand fork of the canyon is strewn evidence of coal mining days: black lumps of coal, sheds, tramway cars, and other discarded pieces of equipment. The several sets of railway tracks, passing dramatically under the immense "tipple," or coal sorting plant, were the town's lifelines in the days when thousands of tons a day were being shipped out.

There is no marker to tell where Spring Canyon changes into Standardville. But, although the canyon becomes narrower and narrower, you can keep going for miles, passing the store and post office, more mining equipment, and many vacant houses —some containing furniture, broken pianos, and other relics. Remember, though, that the whole area is privately owned, and sometimes determinedly patrolled. If you like souvenirs, the most representative is one nobody will miss: a little nugget of coal.

SANTA CLAUS appears to have left his easy chair outside one of the houses in Standardville's narrow canyon.

SPOOKY SCENE at Spring Canyon's long defunct company store seems accentuated by the appearance of a lone figure, one of the town's last remaining residents.

THE RAILROAD was a vital factor in the development of coal mining towns, and Spring Canyon, Utah, was no exception.
In this old "tipple," or coal sorting plant, the coal was first graded, then loaded downward into gondola cars waiting on the
spur track at extreme right.

VARIED STYLES suggest varied eras in these ghost town details.
Above: deeply grained, square-hewn log joints typical of the earliest
period of Montana mining camps. Far right, above: one of the ornaments
of the cast-iron frontal pillars of the Miner's Union Hall, Granite,
Montana. Ordered from hundreds of miles away at great expense,
these pillars express the civic pride and pooling of capital which came
with the hard-rock mining booms later in the century. Far right, below:
wallpaper from the same building, ordered out of a mail order catalogue
from the East. Right: the precisely sawn lumber and standardized
hardware of a company boarding house at Ohio City, Colorado,
probably dating from the turn of the century or later.

Telltale Details: INTIMATE PRESENCE OF THE PAST

The closer you get, the more you see. Grains of time and wood. Scrap of curtain: how glad she was to get it! Battered nail, shoe-worn steps. News of the day stuck up against a Rocky Mountain winter: you can still read the fine print. Bring a close-up camera and take home your own impression.

Tourist Towns: PROMOTING WHOOPEE

Up and down the Rockies the pianos are playing, the donkeys are braying, the little trains are whistling, the barkers are barking. See your name in headlines, catch a jeep tour of the hinterlands. Gold, guns, garters, and ghosts: there's no legend like it.

THE LOWLY DONKEY has come into his own in several of Colorado's mining camps-cum-tourist towns, which now feature yearly burro races. This one is departing from Central City—and you wouldn't believe how fast they go!

WHEN IS A GHOST TOWN not a ghost town? When it advertises free parking. Central City, Colorado, has come back from limbo with gusto, sprucing up its fine old buildings and offering tourists every sort of amenity.

*SQUIRT OR TWO helps to fire up the
resuscitated narrow gauge railway which
leaves Cripple Creek, Colorado, goes out
into the hills, and comes back again.
The former bonanza camp also features a
restored bordello, replete with mannikins.*

LESS FAMOUS than the Comstock Lode, Park City's silver mines actually surpassed the Comstock's by paying out some $400 million after 1872. A sleepy semi-ghost, the Utah town (above and left) is slowly transforming itself into a skiing center in the winter, a tourist town in the summer—but with plenty of ghostly old buildings left over.

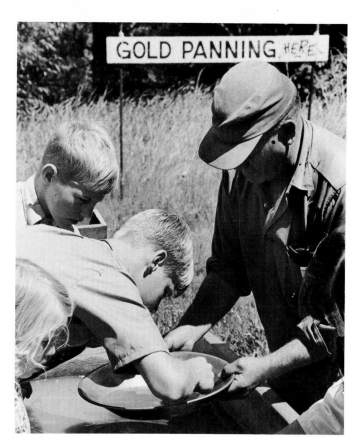

YOUTHFUL GOLD BUGS get the word from an old hand at Virginia City, Montana. In its own madcap youth, the town attracted ten thousand gold seekers and became a "string town," stretching 17 miles along Alder Gulch, where the paydirt was.

STROLL along the boardwalk in Virginia City, Montana, and find yourself immersed in yesterdays. The wild mining camp became a ghost—and is now a veritable museum.

CULTURE CAME to Breckenridge, Colorado, in the form of books, pictures, a piano, and furnishings—all hauled across the plains from the East. When the easily worked placer gold petered out, Breckenridge took to dredging, then became a ghost, and has recently been revived as a vaction home center.

A Personal Touch: REFINING THE RAGTAG CAMPS

As the mining camp grew more substantial, its mounting spirit of civic pride was matched by a new sense of domesticity. Hauled from back East on the brand-new railroad, many a fancy item would have to be abandoned when the town died. But the homemaking spirit, once kindled, had come West to stay.

RELICS ON DISPLAY in old mining camps were once precious luxuries to frontier homemakers. The calendar clock can be seen in Georgetown, Colorado; the fluting iron and chair-of-convenience, in Virginia City, Montana.

Measure of the Past: STRUCTURES WORTH SAVING

Dotted across the West, certain ghost town buildings are worthy of special architectural note. To help preserve them, the National Park Service, together with the Library of Congress, have commissioned careful drawings and other records, assuring these frail spirits a measure of immortality.

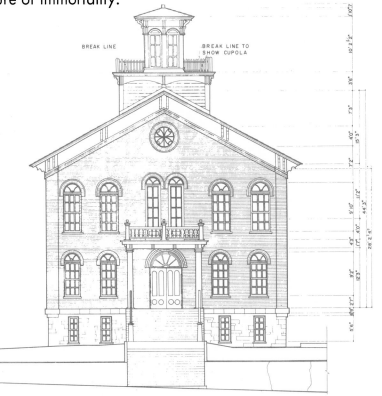

MOST SOPHISTICATED "ghost town" building in Montana—and possibly in the entire West—is Virginia City's Madison County Courthouse (above), still in use. The set of measured drawings commissioned by the Historical American Buildings Survey includes various elevations as well as a number of detail drawings, plus photographs and thoroughly researched historical information. Right: Fraternity Hall, Elkhorn, Montana (see also photos, front cover and page 120).

SHEET METAL FACIA

COMMON BRICK FRONT,
HEADER BOND EVERY
8TH COURSE - WOOD
CASING FOR WINDOWS

GRANITE

SHEET METAL FACIA

COLORED GLASS IN
SMALL SQUARES

CAST IRON COLUMN
COVERS. SEE
SHEET 9 FOR
DETAILS

WOOD PANELS

1890

MINERS UNION
HALL

¼" PLATE
GLASS

THIRD FLOOR

SEE SHEET
NO. 4
DETAIL A

SECOND FLOOR

FIRST FLOOR

5'-4"

11'-9"

12'-9"

44'-8"

14'-10"

SOLID AS A ROCK, the Miners' Union Hall is the only building of note still standing in Granite, Montana. Like the other structures on these pages, it was measured and drawn for posterity by John N. DeHaas, Professor of Architecture at Montana State University.

Georgetown's Hotel de Paris AND THE AMAZING MONSIEUR DUPUY

Of all the surviving examples of elegance in the frontier mining towns, Louis Dupuy's "Hotel de Paris" in Georgetown is perhaps the most captivating. It was a highly individual creation—an island of warm, old-world grace, shadowed by some of the highest peaks in America.

At a time when the fortune hunters of the world were converging on the American West, Dupuy's own story was as unusual as anyone's. Christened Adolphus Gerard about 1844, he ran away from a Normandy theological seminary to become an agnostic intellectual and an apprentice to one of the leading chefs in Paris. He squandered his inheritance, then tried journalism in Paris, London, and New York, where he finally sold two plagiarized essays for $30. But the editor quickly discovered the hoax and chased him downstairs, shouting, "Stop! Thief!"

Gerard next joined the U.S. Army. In Wyoming he deserted, changed his name to Louis Dupuy, got a job in Denver as a mining camp reporter, and headed into the mountains with a burro named Fleurette. He quit to go into the mines—and was badly injured in an explosion. And so Louis became a cook again. Eventually he was able to buy the little Georgetown bakery-cafe where he worked, gradually enlarging it until, in 1875, he opened the doors of his hotel.

For the next 25 years the small establishment was famous throughout the West for its French cuisine and furnishings, and above all for the Dupuy personality. Cloaking his past in fanciful tales, he suavely seated his guests at small, candlelit tables around a tiny Italian fountain and offered them such delicacies as ptarmigan and quail, elk and venison, French mushrooms and truffles, and the finest European wines. Frontier dining had come a long way! After dinner, Louis liked to show off his massive library and treat his guests to an eloquent discourse on philosophy and art.

But he was also cantankerous. After suffering through an unrequited love affair, Louis became a woman-hater. He often turned away female guests, as he did anyone else who did not appeal to him. Yet for 20 years he kept as a "guest," Madame Galet, a French woman much older than himself. Their exact relationship remains a mystery, but she had her room on the second floor and did the housework, and gradually took over the running of the Hotel. She inherited it when Dupuy died in 1900, but was buried beside him five months later.

Long closed to business, the Hotel de Paris has survived almost intact. It is now only an hour's drive from Denver. In the basement is Louis' wine cellar. The ground floor includes plush parlors, the fine library, the remarkably elegant dining room, and the large, typically French kitchen. Upstairs, the bedrooms are decorated with more restraint. The Colonial Dames of Denver own and show the place, with a personal touch which would doubtless have pleased old Louis, who, at his Hotel's opening, told his guests, "Gentlemen: I love these mountains and I love America, but you will pardon me if I bring into this community a remembrance of my youth and my country . . . this house will be my tomb—and if, in after years, someone comes and calls for Louis Dupuy, show them this little souvenir of Alençon which I built in America, and they will understand."

NICETIES of life chez Louis included the bridal suite's richly brocaded bedspread, and unique, very French, corner basins in virtually every room, including downstairs lobbies.

PRECIOUS mementoes, Louis' desk, clock, pictures, and other objects occupy the same corner of the parquet-floored dining room as they did a century ago. Heart of the Hotel, though, was its kitchen, where Louis prepared his gourmet meals in French pots on two charcoal stoves (right).

Hotel de Paris and Restaurant Dining Rooms.

ORDER BILL OF FARE.

*Georgetown,_____187_*

Porter House Steak -	75	Tenderloin Steak -	60
" " wit Onions -	85	" " with Onions	70
" " with Mushrooms 1.00		" " with Mushr'ms,	70
Sirloin Steak -	40	Veal Cutlet -	40
" " with Onions -	50	" Breaded	50
" " with Mushrooms -	70	Mutton Chops -	40
Ham -	40	Pork Steak -	40

FRIED.

Breakfast Bacon -	25	Liver with Salt Pork -	40
Mackerel -	85	Ham and Eggs -	40
Sausage -	85	Pigs Feet -	40
Tripe -	85	Brains -	40

GAME.   FISH.

EGGS.

Boiled -	25	Ham Omelet -	40
Fried -	25	Cheese Omelet -	40
Scrambled -	25	Jelly Omelet -	50
Poached on Toast -	25	Rum Omelet -	50
Omelet, Plain -	25	Mushroom Omelet -	60

MISCELLANEOUS.

Cold Roast Beef -	25	Apple Fritters -	25
Cold Ham -	25	Bread and Milk -	25
Cold Tongue -	24	Mush and Milk -	25
Pigs Feet, Pickled -	30	Welsh Rarebit -	25
Pickled Tripe -	85	Milk Toast -	25

Wheat Cakes -	10	Coffee, per cup -	10
Corn Cakes -	10	Tea, -	10
Buckwheat Cakes -	10	Milk, per glass -	10
Toast -	10	French Chocolate -	25

POTATOES, 10c.

All orders above 25 cents are furnished with Bread, Butter and Potatoes

HOTEL DE PARIS AND Restaurant Dining Rooms.

ORDER BILL OF FARE.

OYSTERS.

Half Doz. Raw.	-	35c.	One Doz. Raw, -	65c.
Half Doz. Stew,	-	40c.	One Doz. Stew, -	75c.
Half Doz. Fried,	-	50c.	One Doz. Fried, -	80c.
Coffee,	- -	10c.	Milk, per Glass, -	10c.
Tea,	- -	10c.	French Chocolate, -	25c.

PRESENTING oysters in the middle of the Rockies was no mean feat in the 1870's. Not listed here were Louis' other specialties, which often included exotic game dishes. He kept his perishables in a huge icebox (above left). After dinner, Louis would entertain his guests in his library or in the sumptuous lobby (left).

GEORGETOWN, COLORADO
FLOWERING OF VICTORIANA

a GHOST TOWN worth seeing

From Denver, take U.S. 6 (Interstate 70) for about forty-eight miles west to Georgetown. The ghost town of Silver Plume, set in the same dramatic mountain canyon, is about two miles farther.

Victorian opulence reached its zenith in the towns built by Colorado's silver booms. The early, flush years of placer gold were quickly followed in the mid-sixties by a slack period. Then the railroad came to Denver, making smelting more practicable; and at the same time there was a widening series of silver strikes.

Georgetown was one of the first beneficiaries of these strikes. In a few years over a hundred million dollars in precious minerals poured out of the surrounding mountains. But in 1893 silver prices suddenly plummeted, and Georgetown's mines were doomed.

The town shrank but did not die. Unique in the Rockies, Georgetown was a mining town of tidy homes rather than of rowdy commerce. Also unique is the fact that it never suffered a major fire—to which it owes its remarkably good state of preservation today. No ghost town, Georgetown is trim and well maintained; it is analogous to Nevada City, California, as an example of the gentility of a few of the late-booming mining communities. In addition to the Hotel de Paris (see preceding pages), Georgetown's highlights include the Maxwell House, which is considered one of the finest examples of Victorian architecture in America; and the Hamill House, containing such elegant appointments as silver and gold wallpaper, diamond-dust mirrors, a curved-glass conservatory, and even a fancy outhouse.

BOLD REMINDER that Georgetown meant business when it came to fire-fighting is the fine old firehouse (above). This mining town was one of the few which never suffered a major conflagration, and one factor was its crack fire brigade (right), which twice won the State Championship.

LOVINGLY CARED FOR, Georgetown's Maxwell House is considered one of the finest Victorian structures in America.

WHAT TIMES they were! The wonderful strawberry festival was barely over in Glenwood, Colorado (above), than the ladies of DeLamar, Idaho (top right), began unlimbering their petticoats for the Fourth-of-July foot race. Yet all this was as nothing compared to the allurements of Potato Day in Carbondale, Colorado (top left). Oh, if we could only know what tickled the picnicking misses at Boulder (right)! And that birthday party at booming Basalt, Colorado (far right)! People nowadays just don't know what a good time is.

Ladies Had Their Day: BOOMTOWN BUTTONS AND BOWS

For liberation they came West where they were scarcer and freer. One became a justice of the peace, another a stagecoach robber. They felt free to change mates, and they made the men change their shirts. Imposing Victorian values, they smoothed the rough edges of mining camp life.

LADIES' AID ➤

BIRTHDAY PARTY.

I. O. O. F. Hall, Monday, May 18, 1896.

••••

A Birthday Party, we're talking about,
And we could not bear to leave YOU out!
So we ask you kindly to come and see
The tip-top time, we'll furnish you free!
We promise to give you supper and song,
So please, dear friend, come right along.
We send you the cutest little sack
And we only ask you to bring it back,
Or send it, if you cannot come,
With as many cents as you are years old.
We promise your age shall never be told!

LADIES' AID.

...LADIES HAD THEIR DAY

"SAY, MARY McGOVERN," said Hannah McGovern, "let's you and me start ourselves up a high-class dry goods establishment." And it came to pass—in Virginia City, Montana, where many such antique establishments are still on view. It isn't certain whether the lady in the photo is Hannah or Mary.

A LADY'S FANCY

DRESS-UP PURSE

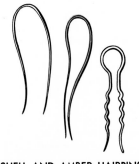

SHELL AND AMBER HAIRPINS

FANCY GARTER

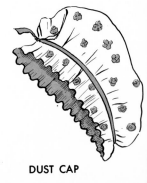

DUST CAP

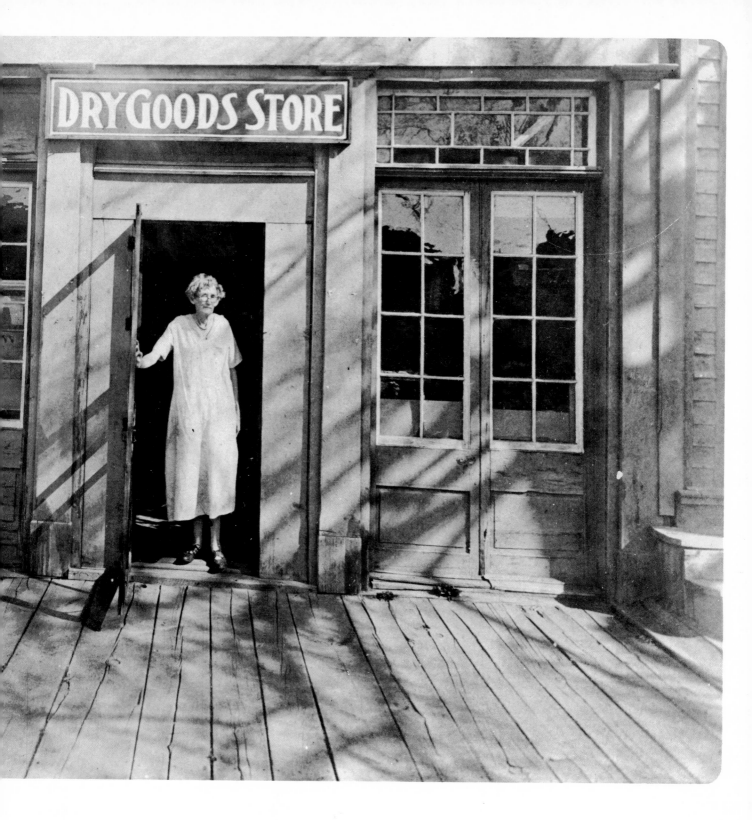

KID-AND-CLOTH SHOE

DRESS-UP BONNET

BEAUTIFICATION was a pathetic and frustrating business for the calico-clad woman of the early frontier. But urban trappings came quickly to the gold and silver towns; and to her hoop skirts, hip bustles, and smelling salts a lady could soon add some precious extras.

Tragic Mementoes: THE SORROWS OF SCOFIELD

Southeast of Salt Lake City lies the former coal mining town of Scofield, Utah. A somnolent shell of its former self, Scofield hardly qualifies as a true ghost town. But its graveyard is special. Here lie the victims of one of the worst disasters in the history of American mining.

WINTER CLOAKS the grave yard at Scofield, Utah, where victims of the coal mine explosion lie buried (right). An unknown photographer recorded the burial scene in 1900 (below). Two hundred men were killed, leaving one hundred seven widows.

ALTA, COLORADO (Southwest of Ouray off U.S. 550; near Telluride on State 145; go southeast from junction near San Miguel River about 8 mi. to New Ophir; take unpaved road northeast about 10 mi.). For ghost-towners who don't mind a steep, rough road, an authentic gem. Fine boarding house (sometimes inhabited by bears) and many houses dot the precipitous forest slopes. More mining camp than town, Alta never had a church, was born in the 1870's, lived intermittently through World War II. Nearby Telluride, Ouray, Silverton are remnants of mining days. From Silverton a delightful narrow-gauge railway carries tourists through spectacular mountain scenery to Durango.

CRESTED BUTTE, COLORADO (North of Gunnison; on State 135). Although no ghost, this one-time coal-mining town recalls its varied past with several old buildings of real character, a number of unprepossessing old dwellings, and such conscious reawakenings as craft shops and a summer theater. Popular with the young crowd, Crested Butte is still isolated enough to keep it off main tourist avenues. Its greatest asset is the magnificent setting—a high valley ringed with mountain peaks.

VICTOR, COLORADO (West of Colorado Springs; south of U.S. 24 on State 67; 6 mi. past Cripple Creek). Easily reached, this extensive partial ghost has a more genuine atmosphere of faded spendor than Cripple Creek. The gold was rich and plentiful, turning up in back yards, under a hotel, in a schoolyard; Victor's streets are literally paved with low-grade ore. Scene of some of the worst labor strife in American history, this stoutly-built city declined from a population exceeding 35,000 in the nineties to around 500 today. Gently rolling, open, mostly treeless country.

SILVER PLUME, COLORADO (West of Denver on Interstate 70, two mi. past Georgetown). More truly a ghost than nearby Georgetown (see page 152), Silver Plume retains a surprisingly off-the-beaten-track air despite its proximity to the main highway. High-quality granite was produced here, as well as silver and gold, lead, zinc, and copper. After the peak years of the 1870's, Silver Plume declined gradually to its present sleepy state, with rows of sagging storefronts, a fine old bandstand beside the river, and a two-story schoolhouse transformed into a museum.

SAINT ELMO, COLORADO (Northwest of Salida; west of U.S. 285 on State 162). Rows of modest, false-fronted buildings mingle with weatherbeaten vacation cabins, all presided over by benevolent camp operator-storekeeper in radio-equipped Scout. Striking location at junction of five gulches and four ore-bearing mountains. Town thrived in the 1880's and '90's not only from its own mines, but also as a stage and railway station to other, larger mining areas, and as a "Saturday-night town." For the intrepid buff, there are two lesser ghosts—Romley and Hancock—farther up the canyon.

The Rockies

GRANITE, MONTANA (Northwest of Anaconda; 4 mi. east of Philipsburg). Pure, very lonely ghost. The 1875 silver bonanza ended in 1893 as 3,000 residents left in 24 hours. Revived in 1898, mines worked until 1958. Starkly impressive Miner's Union Hall is only important building left in town, but there are also old mine buildings in the area, many posted. Steep, short, unpaved road, precipitous mountains, dramatic views.

MARYSVILLE, MONTANA (Northwest of Helena; off State 279). Easily reached partial ghost, sleepy and uncommercial. Spawned by discovery of famous Drumlummon lode in 1876, became Montana's leading gold producer in 1880's and '90's. Two churches, a schoolhouse, brick and stone commercial buildings, residences, and the Drum Lummon mine, all with genuine charm. Lady operating general store is very willing to reminisce about bygone years, show off memorabilia including fine display counters. Many Marysville artifacts are now on display at Historical Society in Helena.

IDAHO'S COEUR d'ALENE AREA (Southeast of Spokane and Coeur d'Alene town; along and just north of Interstate 90). Of considerable importance in the expansion of the Rocky Mountain mining frontier after 1882, this region contains historic mines and several small towns of the period, making a logical tourist loop. Gem, Burke, and Murray will be of the greatest interest to ghost town purists, as well as Osburn, Pritchard, Wardner, and Eagle City. Mining buffs will want to tour the Sunshine, America's largest producing silver mine, located two miles south of Kellogg; also the Bunker Hill Smelter, two miles west of Kellogg.

CASTLE, MONTANA (North of Livingston southeast of junction U.S. 89 & 12). Pure ghost. Silver town, born in the 1880's, killed by demonetization in 1893. Calamity Jane ran a restaurant here. Well-grouped assortment of one- and two-story frame buildings—mainly residential, in various stages of collapse—surrounded by weed-grown, gently rolling hillsides worth exploring for scattered remnants.

SOUTH PASS CITY, WYOMING (South of Lander; east of U.S. 187; off State 28). Careful restoration makes this Wyoming's best ghost. Located near a key Continental Divide crossing on the old Oregon trail, South Pass flared briefly as a bonanza town in the late 1860's, then died when the placers gave out and never participated in the hard-rock era. Most famous resident was Esther Hobart Morris, female justice of the peace who lobbied Wyoming's Territorial Legislature into adopting the world's first women's suffrage act. Log-and-lumber buildings; easy access; roads wind through low, scrubby hills far from civilization.

LIKE ANTS lured to an open jar of honey, "sourdough" prospectors labored over Alaska's treacherous Chilkoot Pass to reach the Klondike gold fields in 1898. Within two years the rush was over, and the roaring Klondike camps joined earlier northwestern boomtowns in heading rapidly toward ghost town status.

PACKERS ASCEND
COPYRIG

IT OF CHILKOOT PASS.

4

THE NORTHWEST WAS SOMETHING ELSE

1858...

IN THE FAR-FLUNG, geographically varied Northwest, the precious ores seemed distributed according to no discernible plan. The high hopes of pioneering prospectors were answered by no bonanza on the scale of a Central City or a Comstock. There occurred, instead, a series of lesser, isolated mining excitements. Widely scattered in space and time, and lacking any one clear trend, these moderate booms left a legacy of fascinatingly diverse ghost towns.

One early strike led to the "Cariboo Country" mania. In the spring of 1858, rumors of gold in the Fraser River area of British Columbia reached California. Suddenly the docks of San Francisco were groaning under the feet of thousands of miners waiting for ships to take them north. But within six months, most of the Argonauts returned, saying there wasn't enough gold in those remote woods to justify spending a long, freezing winter there. And yet there· were eventually enough good-sized discoveries on both sides of the Canadian border to produce, in time, some fine relics of mining-camp days, such as the restored ghost town of Barkerville, B.C.

In 1862, southern Idaho flared into prominence when miners working the Rocky Mountains to the north got wind of a fabulous strike in the Boise Basin. Hurrying down, they impressed Hubert Bancroft, the great historian of the day, as the most footloose of a footloose breed: "The miners of Idaho were like quicksilver. A mass of them dropped in any locality, broke up into individual globules, and ran off after any atom of gold in their vicinity." Center of the latest storm was the new town of Idaho City, which boasted two hundred fifty business buildings by 1865. Though it suffered four major fires, and though the "boomers" dug up the very streets and undermined the buildings in their frenetic search, Idaho City has survived as one of the most touristed of the State's former mining camps.

Scarcely a year after the Boise Basin rush, there were new discoveries a few miles farther south, in the Owyhee Basin. Out of this ferment grew the famous Silver City, whose graceful setting and extensive assortment of carpenter-gothic and other structures make Silver one of the finest ghost towns in all of the West.

Also in 1862, other Argonauts, rushing eastward across Oregon on their way to Idaho's gold fields, stumbled onto paydirt in the John Day area of northeastern Oregon. Within weeks, five thousand more of them came pouring in, to uncover an estimated $26 million in placer gold. Gradually this boom widened to include the Blue Mountains to the east, with the result that Oregon's thinly populated northeastern quadrant now holds the State's richest deposit of ghost towns.

By contrast, Washington was one of the least fortunate western states in terms of gold and silver resources. Washington's small-scale mining flurries occurred mainly in a north-central area adjoining the Canadian frontier. Here there are still a few former mining camps and abandoned homesteads of interest to ghost-town buffs.

Last of the major western mining rushes, the Klondike stampede of 1898 was also one of the briefest and most hectic. As many as a hundred thousand "sourdough" prospectors set out to cross Alaska's frozen wastes for the Yukon bonanza camp of Dawson. The harsh environment gave this gold rush a tough character, which is still evident in the region's partially abandoned way stations and defunct mining camps.

In the great and scattered Northwest, there can be few overall directions for ghost-towning. Winters, of course, can be severe. Considerable distances separate one region from another, so it's wise to explore one area thoroughly, rather than trying to encompass the scattered whole. Many of the ghost towns of Oregon, Washington, and Canada are in or near forests, with excellent prospects for fishing, hunting, and game watching. However, if you're traveling the Forest Service roads, reliable local advice and detailed, small-scale maps are a necessity.

THE NORTHWEST AND ITS GHOST TOWNS

✗ True Ghost Town: Majority of buildings disused; few if any residents; no modern facilities.

✷ Partial Ghost Town: Some disused buildings; some residents; limited facilities.

★ Tourist Ghost Town: Old structures refurbished to promote old-time atmosphere; modern facilities.

🛡40 Interstate Highways

🛡80 U.S. Highways

95 State Highways & Secondary Roads

NOTE: Map is as accurate as present information permits. Refer to detailed maps for minor roads, and always inquire locally about road conditions.

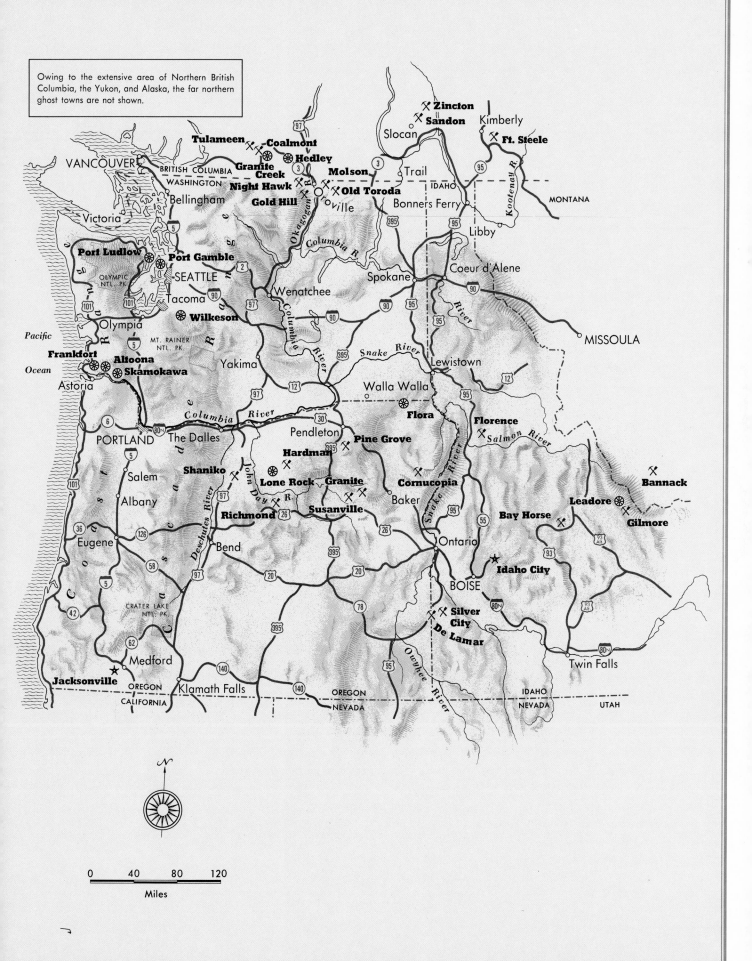

Owing to the extensive area of Northern British Columbia, the Yukon, and Alaska, the far northern ghost towns are not shown.

VANCOUVER

BRITISH COLUMBIA
WASHINGTON

Tulameen
Coalmont
Granite Creek
Hedley
Night Hawk
Molson
Old Toroda
Gold Hill
Oroville

Zincton
Sandon
Kimberly
Slocan
Ft. Steele
Trail
IDAHO
MONTANA

Bellingham

Victoria

Kootenay R.

Port Ludlow
Port Gamble
SEATTLE

OLYMPIC NTL. PK.

Tacoma

Wilkeson

Olympia

MT. RAINER NTL. PK.

Pacific

Ocean

Frankfort
Altoona
Skamokawa
Astoria

Yakima

Wenatchee

Columbia R.

Spokane

Bonners Ferry

Libby

Coeur d'Alene

MISSOULA

Snake River

Lewistown

Walla Walla

Columbia River

The Dalles

PORTLAND

Salem

Albany

Eugene

Bend

Shaniko

Richmond

Pendleton

Hardman

Lone Rock

Granite

Susanville

Pine Grove

Cornucopia

Baker

Flora

Florence

Salmon River

Bannack

Leadore

Gilmore

Bay Horse

Ontario

Idaho City

BOISE

Silver City

De Lamar

Twin Falls

Medford

Jacksonville

OREGON
CALIFORNIA

Klamath Falls

OREGON
NEVADA

IDAHO

NEVADA

UTAH

Owyhee River

Deschutes River

John Day R.

Coast Range

Cascade Range

Cascade Range

Coast Range

N

0   40   80   120

Miles

BANNACK, MONTANA
"TU GRASS HOP PER DIGGINS 30 MYLE"

a GHOST TOWN worth seeing

From Salmon, Idaho (on U.S. 93 about one hundred twenty miles south of Missoula) go southeast twenty-two miles on State 28 to Tendoy. Turn east on an unsurfaced road which becomes Montana State 324. Just beyond Grant, approximately fifteen miles from Bannack, turn north.

VACANT seats await worshippers who no longer appear in Bannack's Methodist Church, built in 1870.

Lewis and Clark journeyed by canoe through the upper Missouri and Beaverhead Valleys in 1805, and in their wake came a few trappers. But it remained for a little band of miners on their way from Colorado to Idaho in 1862 to make the first significant gold strike at the western edge of the territory later to be called Montana. Dubbing their site "Grasshopper Diggins," they decided to build log cabins and stay through the winter. When others joined them, the mining camp of Bannack was born. A year later, its deposits of both placer and quartz gold proved so valuable that Bannack soon boasted more than three thousand residents. Yet the town was still so hard to find that one resident scrawled the above directions on a sign, adding, "kepe the trale next the bluffe."

Today, Bannack's remarkable structures contain more than a century of colorful history. The little jail, stoutly mortised together out of square-hewn logs, was built by that notorious scalawag, Sheriff Henry Plummer. Pretending to pursue holdup men while actually leading them, Plummer was eventually found out and hanged on his own gallows. The largest building in town, a two-story brick affair, served as the County Seat from 1875 until 1881, then became a hotel. Other historic buildings include the Masonic hall and schoolhouse, built in 1871, and the lovely little frame church, dating from 1870. There are a number of old log cabins, tightly chinked with lime. And don't miss the two graveyards. All in all, Bannack is a classic among western ghost towns.

VINES CREEP through the sagging shutters of a deserted Bannack residence, said to be the first frame house in Montana.

UNUSUAL RECORD of life in a town well on the way to becoming a
ghost, these photographs were taken in Bannack during the 1930's.
The ladies wheel their charges past a tightly chinked, squarehewn
log cabin typical of Montana's earliest mining camps.

WEATHERED FENCE provides the traditional locale for a heart-to-heart housewives' chat. The left building in background is Bannack's picturesque Methodist Church.

OLD CRONIES lounge on the boardwalk, look over a piece of ore, and discuss prospects for reworking the old diggins.

Old Dredges: THE PROFIT SCRAPERS

At the turn of the century, after the "boomers" had abandoned their claims for flashier prospects, the patient dredgers moved in. Some of them prospered quietly for years—then left their huge tailings and bulky equipment dotted across the landscape of the mining West.

DREDGES DIG their way through gold-bearing river gravels, wet and dry. Taking their artificial "lake" with them, they chew away at the bank in front and leave behind continuous mounds, which are sometimes called "earthworms." One or more spuds— pointed steel piles—anchor the dredge and serve as pivots around which it can rotate.

GETTING THE RICHES: THE GOLD DREDGE

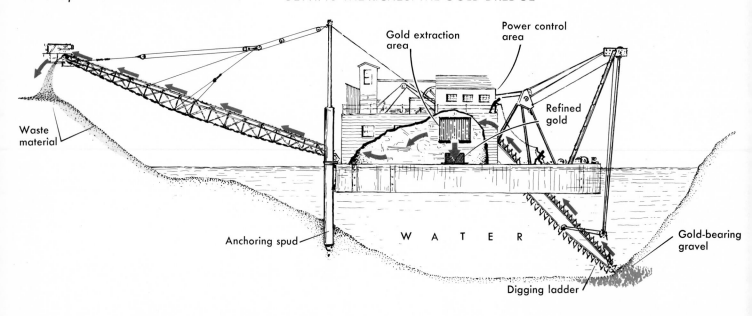

Gold extraction area

Power control area

Refined gold

Waste material

Anchoring spud

WATER

Gold-bearing gravel

Digging ladder

WILLIAMS CREEK, site of the restored ghost town of Barkerville, B.C., was the prime source of more than $50 million in gold taken out in the wake of the "Cariboo" rush of 1861. After the excitement died down, this two-piece dredge and its predecessors worked the Creek's bottom gravels profitably for many years.

MOULDERING in a sump of its own making, this long-abandoned dredge sits in Jordan Creek, between the Idaho ghost towns of Bonanza and Custer.

SILVER CITY, IDAHO
QUIXOTIC QUEEN OF GHOSTS

Both order and gaiety have always pervaded Silver City. Whereas most western mining camps evolved in a helter-skelter manner, Silver was built according to a predetermined plan. In 1863, residents of Ruby City, a mile down Jordan Creek, decided that Ruby was too cold and windy, and too far from their diggings. So Ruby's buildings were gradually transferred up to this cozy canyon. The most imposing of these original structures, the Idaho Hotel, was once brushed by many a petticoat, but is no longer safe to enter. If you venture down the slope behind the hotel, though, you can observe some of Silver's quainter institutions: second-story outhouses perched on stilts and connected to the main buildings by dizzy catwalks, some roofed over to protect patrons against the elements.

When the mines proved rich, Silver City grew explosively. Then, in the usual way of mining camps, its swollen population suddenly shrank to 593. After 1880 the mines revived, and Silver boomed anew. But by the 1940's it had become a true ghost; unfortunately, some of its fine, old buildings were torn down or taken away. Since then, however, at least one die-hard has always stuck around to protect this extensive and delightful ghost, with its many touches of carpenter-gothic.

These days the job falls to Mr. and Mrs. Adams; they'll be happy to take you up to the two-story schoolhouse, whose upper floor they've made into an abundant little museum.

Some of Silver's old houses have recently been reoccupied as vacation residences. And real gaiety returns to this old queen each summer, when the Owyhee County Cattlemen pour in by the hundreds for an annual weekend spree.

a GHOST TOWN worth seeing

From Boise, go sixteen miles west to Nampa on U.S. 30, then twenty-eight miles south to Murphy on State 45. Here, get directions to either of two unpaved roads, both rather rough, leading to town of Silver City.

LOOKING NORTH, you see the Barber Shop and Leonard's Store in the right foreground. The large gray building to right of center is the Masonic Hall; to the left and up the hill is the Catholic Church.

SILVER CITY, IDAHO, 1971

1. Church
2. School
3. Stoddard Mansion
4. Masonic Hall
5. Tin Shop
6. Avalanche Newspaper
7. Idaho Hotel
8. Hotel
9. Bar and Store (still in use)
10. Lippincott Building
11. Post Office
12. Cemetery
13. Chinese Laundry
14. I.O.O.F. Hall
15. Bank
16. Saloon
17. Store
18. Court House
19. Ice House
20. Butcher Shop
21. Leonard's Store
22. Barber Shop
23. Undertaker and Hotel Rooms
24. Miners' Union Hospital

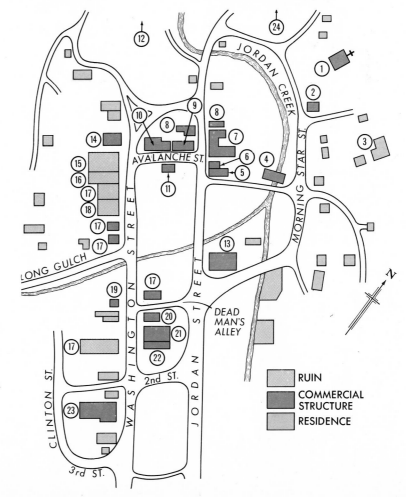

DRESSED UP in their Sunday best—perhaps for a wedding—these good friends pose on the front porch of a Silver City cabin in the days when the town was still very much alive.

BIG-HATTED members of the Owyhee County Cattlemen's Association still gather one weekend a year at Silver City, Idaho, for a little serious business and a lot of hell-raising. Business is handled in the old schoolhouse (below); the rest goes on day and night, wherever the spirits are flowing.

GINGERBREAD of the photogenic
Stoddard house is beginning to
crumble. Entrepreneur J. W.
Stoddard owned mining shares,
a sawmill, and a cattle ranch.

CARPENTER-GOTHIC touches on a number of Silver's quaint buildings were largely the contribution of a craftsman who came to Silver City from Germany.

WHITE SCHOOLHOUSE, now a museum, is framed in this photo by two boarded-up hotels on Jordan Street, Silver's main thoroughfare. Jordan Creek lies below the trees; the cabins, like several others in town, are owned by part-time residents. . .

Bidding farewell to the lives they had known, increasing numbers of Americans undertook the overland trek to Oregon in the late 1830's. The famous Lewis and Clark Expedition had paved the way in 1804-5, and eight years later Robert Stuart, a Scotsman, blazed the more southerly route which would become known as the Oregon Trail. Next came a smattering of trappers, explorers, and missionaries. But not until a nation-wide depression in 1837 left millions nearly destitute were great numbers of settlers spurred to make the arduous journey west. Adding patriotic luster to the promise of free land in Oregon's fertile valleys was the widespread popular belief that it was the nation's "manifest destiny" to expand from sea to shining sea.

In the early 1840's, the trickle of wagons rolling west out of Missouri became a flood. But many of the pioneers were naively ill-prepared for the rigorous journey. Western geography confronted them with extreme challenges, from plunging mountain gorges, where wagons had to be lowered on ropes, to parched deserts, littered with the whited bones of those who hadn't made it. Quicksand claimed the lives of oxen; boulders cracked the wagons' axletrees; torrential rapids threatened to sweep away whole convoys. Dust, insects, wind, snow, and terrifying thunderstorms all added to the strain. Indians were sometimes friendly—often hostile. Buffalo, an important source of meat and hides, sometimes thundered across the plains in dangerous stampedes.

Less obvious, but just as severe, were the human problems. Unprepared for adversity, many immigrants fell to bickering over such questions as who should stand guard at night, or whose family and livestock should drink first at a water hole. Sometimes so much bitterness developed that the wagon train would split into separate groups, traveling miles apart. Strong, knowledgeable leadership was essential to guide the way, to overrule the bickering, and to enforce the one absolute law: keep going!

In their lighter moods, the travelers sang, danced, and prayed around their campfires. Although their five-month, two-thousand-mile journey would leave them exhausted and penniless, they were sustained by the promise of a new and better life ahead. Their rough-hewn optimism, sense of freedom, and capacity for hard work would become key qualities in that newly emergent American, "the Westerner."

DETERMINED to get there, these westering pioneers have paused to let their livestock graze, and to rest their own weary bones from the ceaseless jolting of the covered wagons.

HARDMAN, OREGON
ON AND OFF THE LINE

a GHOST TOWN worth seeing

From Pendleton, go twenty-three miles southwest on U.S. 395, then take State 74 thirty-seven miles to Heppner. Go eleven miles southeast on 206/207, take southern fork (207) another nine miles to Hardman. Alternate route north from Mitchell, on U.S. 26, passes ghost town of Richmond.

Transportation was Hardman's life—and death. From the 1860's on, stagecoaches and freight wagons labored ceaselessly across the plains east of the Cascades, supplying local farmers and miners and carrying their goods to market. Planted in an ocean of wheatfields, with pine forests brooding in the near distance, the little settlement of Dairyville became a favorite stopping point for the freighters and stage drivers. Dairyville became popularly known as "Raw Dog," and less than a mile away a rival settlement sprang up, known as "Yallerdog." At first, in the manner of so many frontier towns, the two struggled fiercely for supremacy. But eventually they amalgamated, to become "Dog Town." In the meantime a nearby farmer named David N. Hardman had been operating the post office out of his house. As the new community prospered and grew, he moved to town, bringing his post office with him. And so Dog Town changed its name again —to Hardman.

From sawmills in the nearby Blue Mountains came a steady supply of board lumber. After 1910, farmers from miles around brought their wheat to be ground in Hardman's big mill. To accommodate free-spending travelers, hotels went up, and when the railroad came puffing into eastern Oregon, everyone naturally assumed Hardman would be on the line.

But they were wrong, and as staging and wagon freighting inevitably declined, so did Hardman. Today, horses and sheep meander through its vacant streets, grazing in former front yards. Hens cluck angrily at unfamiliar visitors. Yet the post office that prompted Dog Town to change its name struggles on, and it is now included within the one sleepy little general store which comprises Hardman's sole remaining business establishment.

JUMBLE of frame structures, some intermittently occupied, comprise Hardman. Free-ranging animals add to the atmosphere of strangeness.

WARMING in the light of early morning, Hardman's Odd Fellows Hall rests beside the endless plains whose wheat once brought prosperity to the town.

PLUNGING across the rich wheatfields of
eastern Washington, a twenty-seven-horse
team pulls a harvesting combine. In the
nineteenth century, farming prospered east
of the Cascades at first, but then declined,
leaving agricultural ghost towns.

The Land Bloomed: LIFE AND DEATH OF FARM TOWNS

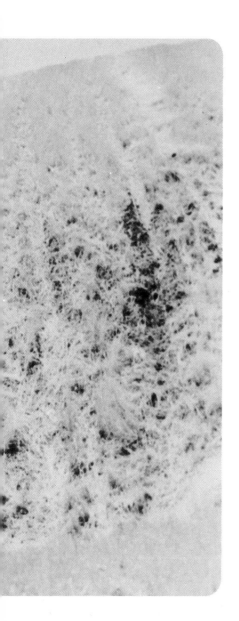

If mining was the dynamite of western expansion, farming was its wheel and axle. The cry, FREE LAND! drew thousands of immigrants to Oregon Territory in the 1840's and 50's. As the century progressed, agriculture rivaled mining as the West Coast's leading enterprise.

Many of the farmers had moved more than once. They had left New England's exhausted fields to settle in the Middle Atlantic States or Midwest, then pulled up stakes again to join the westering wagon trains. Many who pursued the Oregon Trail came to the rich Willamette Valley, near Portland. Although Oregon lost two-thirds of her adult male population to California's gold rush, Willamette agriculture boomed as hundreds of ships raced up from San Francisco, offering high prices for food. Wheat, previously declared a form of legal tender at a dollar a bushel, skyrocketed to six dollars a bushel.

After 1861 good Willamette land was becoming scarce, and wheat farmers followed the miners to the rolling plains of central and eastern Oregon. With the Columbia River providing a natural shipping lane, the movement quickly spread to eastern Washington, where the number of farms tripled in ten years. The coming of the railroads in the 1880's gave the farmers a further boost.

By the 1870's the cattlemen, too, were discovering good lands east of the Cascades.

Many brought herds west over the Oregon Trail to these ranges, where the bunch grass grew stirrup-high and the cattleman was king—until the sheepherder arrived. Then came bitter range warfare, complicated by the appearance of land speculators and homesteaders.

But just when big-time promoters were starting to plan whole new agricultural communities, negative signs appeared: overproduction, uncertain market conditions, and two severe winters, which wiped out several herds and discouraged many farmers. One of them quipped:

> If I can make enough in time
> To take me out of this cold clime
> You bet your life I'll stomp away
> From Oregon and the John Day.

Soon the farmers saw their sons lured away to new enterprises in the rich forests and expanding cities. In the ten years after 1880, Oregon's farms dropped in value from about fifty percent to twenty-seven percent of the State's assessed wealth. The trend in eastern Washington was the same. And after the turn of the century, new waves of homesteaders, journeying from the East to eastern Oregon, found it impossible to live off the land, and either turned back or pushed on to the coast.

So it happened that agriculture, although not so fickle a mistress as mining, created some ghost towns of its own.

CLASSIC FIGURES,
immigrant farmers toil the Oregon
soil. The rich Willamette Valley
was the destination for thousands
of farmers whose eastern lands
had become nearly exhausted.

SHANIKO, OREGON
GONE TO SEED

a GHOST TOWN worth seeing

From The Dalles, go eighteen miles east on Interstate 80, then south on U.S. 97, fifty-seven miles to Shaniko, the center of which lies several hundred yards east of the highway. Antelope, eight miles farther south, is sometimes erroneously listed as a ghost town; Grandview, Geneva and Howard, sixty miles farther south, are more obscure minor ghosts. Get directions to Grandview and Geneva at Culver; to Howard at Prineville.

Today, Shaniko is a virtual ghost. Its only remaining life centers around the rustic, two-story Shaniko Hotel, where all twenty-seven rooms are occupied by old-age pensioners—spirited souls who still enjoy telling you about "the good old days."

Shaniko's own good old days began in the 1870's, when a German immigrant named August Scherneckau bought a sleepy stagecoach stop called Cross Hollows, on the line between The Dalles and Canyon City. Profiting on the then-expanding wheat and livestock industries, he built a store, hotel, and blacksmith shop. A few years later, Scherneckau moved away to Astoria and then to California, where he died.

In the 1880's and 90's, sheep ranching became so important in this plateau country that, in 1900, railroad entrepreneurs from The Dalles ran a line south in order to ship the raw wool up to the Columbia River port of Biggs Junction. To serve the needs of the busy rail head, they laid out a full-fledged town a short distance from Cross Hollows, christening it "Shaniko" after the local Indians' way of pronouncing the name of the German immigrant they still remembered.

Shaniko soon hummed with activity. Spring water was pumped over from Cross Hollows and stored in a picturesque wooden water tower, which you can still see. Other structures, built around the turn of the century and still on view, include a combination city hall, fire house, and jail; an unusual schoolhouse; a general store; and a number of lesser buildings housing fine displays of antique wagons, carriages, and automobiles.

By 1910 Shaniko had reached the zenith of its prosperity and was digging its own grave, as men headquartered here labored to build a new, more level and convenient railroad line along the Deschutes River Canyon. Once this was completed, Bend was substituted for Shaniko as the shipping point, and the little town, having lost its purpose, faded fast.

NOWHERE is the destination of most of Shaniko's boardwalks, but some of the resident pensioners take walks on them anyway.

DISTINCTIVE schoolhouse, built in 1902, stands alone some distance from the center of town.

Oroville's Orbit: GHOST TOWNS OF NORTHERN WASHINGTON

Washington's north-central area once played host to a series of small gold mining booms. Now the ghosts of those forgotten excitements mingle with the spirits of many another deserted homestead and cabin in this thinly populated stretch along the Canadian border.

MOSS gathers on an abandoned log cabin near Old Toroda, in Washington's Okanogan National Forest, southeast of Oroville.

TYPICAL LOG CABIN CORNERS

VARIETY of notching styles appeared in log cabins throughout the West as a result of mingling cultural influences and the Yankee habit of improvising. Some structures even had two different types of notches.

SADDLE NOTCH, TOP AND BOTTOM

QUAINT gold town of Molson, Washington, near the Canadian border, has been reconstituted from old buildings and artifacts found in the surrounding area.

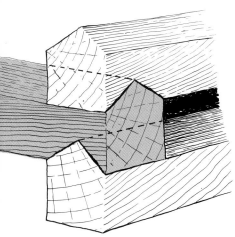

REGULAR V-NOTCH

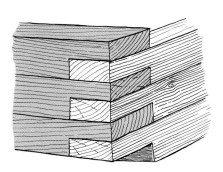

OVERLAPPING HALF-NOTCH

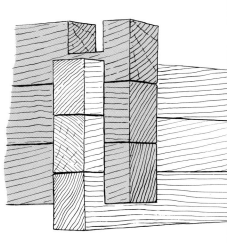

DOUBLE LOCKING NOTCH

BRIGHT fall foliage overtakes an
abandoned cabin near the tiny
ghost town of Old Toroda, tucked
away in Okanogan National
Forest, southeast of Oroville.

MYSTERY SHROUDS these old houses east of Oroville, Washington. In this remote strip just below the Canadian frontier are many abandoned homesteads.

NESTLING against a steep hillside, Zincton
seems camouflaged because many of its
buildings were painted green. A comparatively
recent ghost, Zincton was inhabited
as late as 1951.

MAGNIFICENT WRECK, the old mill at Hedley
dominates a town that is not quite dead. The
surrounding cliffs contain other precariously
perched reminders of mining days.

Kootenay Camps: THE UNSUNG BOOM

Though overshadowed by the glamor of the Fraser River and ''Cariboo'' rushes, the Kootenay area of southern British Columbia was rich in gold, silver, lead, and copper. The Kootenay mines peaked just after the turn of the century, then declined— leaving a smattering of moody ghost towns and abandoned mine works.

DRAMATIC backdrop of Lakit Mountain and the Hughes Range looms behind Fort Steele. This extensive ghost town is being carefully restored.

GLOW of autumn permeates a log dwelling
at Granite Creek. Though it boomed only
from 1885 to about 1912, the gold camp
was then the third largest community
in the Province.

SPLENDOR of fall color is framed in the
punched-out windows of the great ore mill
at Zincton. As its name implies, the town
produced zinc and other base metals.

a GHOST TOWN worth seeing

From Trail, B.C., go thirty-one miles northeast on Prov. 13 to South Slocan, then cut north on Prov. 6, forty-two miles to New Denver. Turn east on gravel road for six miles, then right again on an even poorer road for two miles to Sandon.

Hacked out of the sheer cliff wall, the narrow road snakes north only yards above gleaming Slocan Lake. All around you, snow-capped mountains loom higher and higher. In 1892, a Virginian named Johnny Harris came this way by canoe. When it overturned he made his way up into the rugged mountains on foot—and struck a rich vein of silver. To follow in his footsteps, turn right at the little outpost of New Denver. The unpaved road rises steeply up the forested slopes, then drops down into a dark canyon; you find yourself in Sandon, the town Johnny Harris founded and presided over.

Or what's left of it. The site is strewn with battered planks and logs, and Carpenter Creek churns through what used to be Sandon's downtown. Originally, the main buildings were huddled against the side of the narrow canyon; but in 1900, following a disastrous fire, Harris flumed and narrowed the stream and built boardwalks over it, thus transforming Carpenter Creek into Sandon's main street. Fifty-five years later, with the former mining camp already a virtual ghost, the log-jammed water suddenly burst from its confines, ripping away the boardwalks, upending buildings, undermining others, and scattering wreckage everywhere. Incredibly, some of the buildings survived, and are still well worth seeing.

The twisted, washed-out railroad tracks are relics of the silver boom era, when the Canadian Pacific and Great Northern literally raced one another to complete the first ore-shipping line from Sandon. When the CP won, the GN engineer got so mad he hooked his locomotive to the CP station and yanked it into the creek. Anyway, there was plenty of ore for everyone, and Sandon's population peaked at about 3,000, before falling silver prices and a mad exodus to the Klondike gold rush combined to kill the camp permanently.

SHRINKING Sandon had less and less use for its huge city hall building, so the bottom floor was given over to an elementary school. Now this, too, is totally deserted.

TOWN FATHER Johnny Harris came from Virginia as a prospector, struck it rich in Carpenter Creek, and founded Sandon. After a disastrous fire in 1900, many new structures went up, including Hunter's General Store (left) and Harris' office building, which he named the Virginia Block.

HUDDLING along roaring Carpenter Creek in 1898, Sandon was a perfect fire trap, and two years later fire wiped out more than fifty downtown buildings. The town was rebuilt according to a unique plan that called for boardwalks to cover portions of the creek.

REBUILT after the 1900 fire, most of Sandon's larger buildings were wiped out for good by the 1955 flood. The City Hall was one of the few to survive this second disaster.

RED LIGHT section escaped the raging flood in 1955 because it was built on higher ground, apart from the rest of town.

Signs of the Times: BOOSTING THE BOOMTOWNS

The boisterous individualism of the exploding West
found ready expression in the sign-maker's craft.
Plastered with posters and placards, wallside pitches
and false-front pronouncements, today's wry
ghost towns trumpet their exuberant yesterdays.

BRICK, metal, wood, cardboard, bottle tops—anything would do. Resounding through silent streets, these ghost-town-criers still carry the boisterous accents of the Old West.

GILMORE, IDAHO
THEN AS NOW, RATHER FAR-OUT

Here's a real find—a fairly extensive ghost that hasn't been picked over. The scenery around Gilmore is unusual, too: forested hills rise steeply just behind the town, and camera buffs will appreciate the constantly shifting light in the mountain-rimmed valley.

Gold was discovered here in 1873, and lead and silver were commercially produced as early as 1889. But Gilmore was isolated from the main mining trends and main producing areas, and hauling its heavy ores by mule teams proved a difficult business. One company after another tried and failed. Then, in 1910, the "Gilmore and Pittsburg Railway" was put through, and at last the ore could be transported easily to Montana's major smelting centers. Shipping some twelve million dollars' worth by 1929, the town prospered.

But the Depression killed Gilmore. Today, the aged general store-and-freight office stares bleakly through its shattered front windows, its floors ankle deep with carefully drawn bills, invoices, and other paperwork dating from the roaring twenties. Across the street stands Jaggers Hotel, proudest structure in town. Once the abode of a lonely hermit, Jaggers is now totally abandoned. Widely scattered across the town's gentle grassy slope are some remaining dwellings; a few have part-time occupants. Adventurous visitors may also explore the rutted road behind Gilmore, leading toward the old mine sites.

a GHOST TOWN worth seeing

From Salmon, Idaho, take State 28 forty-five miles southeast to Leadore, which itself has some ghost town elements. Go south another seventeen miles to an unpaved road, sometimes marked "Gilmore," which exits right; the town is about a mile farther up the grassy slope.

DESERTED house (above) is one of many such relics in Gilmore. Right: square-set mining timbers are tumbled about incongruously in the middle of town.

CEASELESS shiftings or weather bring many moods to remote Gilmore. Jaggers Hotel is seen from rear at the center of the picture.

WHETHER your home was an Oregon cabin (far right) or an outpost in the Cariboo country (right), you'd naturally ask the travelling photographer to snap you—and yours—in the doorway.

GLASS PLATE photograph was taken in or near Pendleton, Oregon, toward the turn of the century. Sheep raising had become a major enterprise, and the elegant ladies are probably sitting on blankets made at the new Pendleton Mills. The decline of sheep ranching killed a number of towns but not, of course, the mills.

Family Album: THE PHOTOGRAPHER COMES TO TOWN

By a happy coincidence, the art of photography grew up simultaneously with the mining frontier. Both travelling photographer and local portraitist helped the new towns to celebrate their existence, and to prove to eastern and European relatives that the pioneers were alive and well and living in the West.

PHOTOGRAPHER Peter Britt, one of the best known mining camp portraitists, lived in Jacksonville, Oregon. His studio is reconstructed in the museum of this former gold town which has become a tourist center.

RALLYING POINT of the Yukon rush was the town of Dawson. Founded in 1896, it had 35,000 residents by 1898, but dwindled to 3,000 in 1908. Today it's a virtual ghost, with many old buildings. Winter brings six weeks of total darkness and temperatures as low as —70°.

CATTLE DRIVE down the main street of Barkerville, B.C., brought out plenty of kibitzers in 1868. The gold camp is now one of the best restored ghost towns in the West.

The disgruntled placer miners who returned to California in 1858, ending British Columbia's abortive Fraser River gold rush, did not realize that the big treasure was still waiting—in the Cariboo country to the north, and in the frigid Klondike. When most of the footloose Yankees had gone, the determined British pushed the "Great North Road" into the gold-rich Cariboo. Completed in 1865, this vital link connected the river port of Yale to the fabulous gold camp of Barkerville, almost four hundred miles due north. Today's modern highway follows a nearly identical route and provides fascinating backward glimpses of the boom times. Along the way are lovely early churches, venerable artifacts such as freight wagons, and old "mile houses" which still serve hearty meals. But the prize is Barkerville itself, a meticulously restored tourist ghost town.

In the Klondike, by contrast, the transportation problem was so severe that it was never really overcome. In 1898 the gold seekers fought their way across the frozen wilderness—on foot, by dog team and pack train, by barge and stern-wheeler—from the notorious ocean port of Skagway, Alaska, to the equally wicked boom town of Dawson, deep in the Yukon interior. With food and other supplies precious, the prospectors became known as "sourdoughs" because many kept a culture of old batter behind their cabin stove pipes, ready for the next baking.

Although the monumental efforts of the Klondike hopefuls inspired such writers as Robert Service and Jack London, the statistics tell a grimmer story: "Perhaps one hundred thousand people set out for Dawson, thirty to forty thousand got there, fifteen to twenty thousand prospected, four thousand found some gold, fifteen thousand people out of the year's rush remained in the Klondike when winter closed in, and another five thousand departed before spring came. They spent somewhere between thirty and sixty million dollars for transportation and supplies, yet the yield of gold from the Klondike in 1898 was hardly more than ten million dollars." Though well publicized, the rush was brief: by 1900 it was virtually over.

These days, you can retrace one hundred ten miles of the old route by taking a charming little narrow gauge train from Skagway to Carcross and Whitehorse, all three of which contain interesting mementoes of the gold rush era. Dawson itself is a semi-ghost, with many buildings dating from its wild and wooly heyday.

SOURDOUGHS camping in the Yukon look as tough as they must have been to survive in this fierce environment. Few of them made much on the short-lived rush.

BAY HORSE, IDAHO (Northeast of Stanley; west off U.S. 93 about 14 mi. northeast of Clayton, about 5 mi. on dirt road). A very sleepy little ghost, partly occupied, many of its former buildings now gone. Besides a half dozen or more old structures in varying states of collapse, there are a locked-up old mill, ''beehive'' coke ovens, two cemeteries, an old-time gas pump perched forlornly amid sagebrush, and other memorabilia. After booming in the 1880's and 1890's, the town withered when its silver and lead production fell off, and by World War I Bay Horse had become a ghost. In a steep, rugged, narrow canyon.

WASHINGTON'S ''GHOST COAST'' (*Frankfort,* north of Astoria, Oregon, on river beyond end of logging road which goes east from State 401 between Megler and Naselle; *Skamokawa,* from Interstate 5 at Longview, take State 4 west for 34 mi.; *Altoona* and *Pillar Rock,* from Skamokawa take State 4 west for 13½ mi., then State 403 south 7 mi.; Continue east 4 mi. on gravel road to Pillar Rock; *Knappton* from 403, north of Altoona take State 4 west for 10 mi., then State 401 south for 7½ mi.; *McGowan,* from Knappton go west to north end of Astoria-Megler Toll Bridge but do not cross it, rather continue west onto U.S. 101 for 1½ mi.). Along the lower Columbia, this smattering of rotting buildings marks the booms of the late nineteenth century.

GHOST TOWNS OF NORTH-CENTRAL WASHINGTON (*Nighthawk,* 12 mi. northwest of Oroville on gravel road; *Molson,* from Oroville take Tonasket Creek Road east for 7 mi., then turn north on Mud Lake Valley Road for 6 mi.; *Gold Hill,* get direction at Loomis, 11 mi. west of U.S. 97 from Ellisford; *Old Toroda and Bodie,* at Tonasket, south of Oroville on U.S. 97, take State 30 east for 24 mi. to Wauconda, then 6 mi. northeast on a gravel road to Old Toroada, at the confluence of Cougar and Toroda Creeks— follow the road which parallels Toroda Creek another 9 mi. to Bodie. The best map for roads through this area is the Okanogan National Forest Map which can be purchased from the National Forest Service, a branch of the U.S. Department of Agriculture.) A scattered variety of tiny, true ghosts. Molson comes closest to the usual idea of a ghost town, with false-front buildings and artifacts, plus, in another section, a later vintage of buildings and wrecked autos. Old Toroda and the back roads throughout Okanogan National Forest contain many isolated, abandoned cabins and houses. Terrain around Oroville varies from lush, damp forest to bleak sagebrush hills.

LEADORE, IDAHO (47 mi. southeast of Salmon on State 28). A curious sprawling community, with various ghost town and modern section separated by wide vacant lots. Leadore owed part of its early importanc to the development of Gilmore (page 201) and other nearby minin camps in the Lemhi Valley. The town was also a center for agricultur and ranching supplies. While these functions have declined, Leadore sti gets by as a road stop, its living center appropriately shifted from th original, false-fronted street (see photo) out to the modern highway On a grassy plain surrounded by distant, brooding mountain ranges

GHOST TOWNS OF BRITISH COLUMBIA, YUKON TERRITORY, AND ALASKA (*Ft. Steele,* northeast of Trail, B.C., 12 mi. north of Cranbrook or Prov. 93/95; *Zincton,* north of Trail, on unpaved mountain road between New Denver on Prov. 6 and Kaslo; *Coalmont, Granite Creek,* and *Tulameen,* east of Penticton, 5 mi. northeast of Princeton on gravel mountain road; *Barkerville,* roughly 400 mi. north of Penticton via Can. 1, Prov. 97, and at Quesnel, 65 mi. east on Prov. 26; *Skagway, Alaska, Carcross, Y.T.,* and *Whitehorse, Y.T.,* the three connected by scenic narrow-gauge train, Whitehorse being on Alaskan Highway in Yukon about 120 mi. northwest of B.C. border, Carcross accessible by road, about south of Whitehorse, and Skagway accessible only by air, sea, or aforementioned railway; *Dawson, Y.T.,* east of Fairbanks, Alaska: from Alaskan Highway—State 2—at Tetlin Junction, Alaska, 130 mi. northwest of Canadian Border, take gravel road called ''Taylor Highway'' about 170 mi. northeast, or else by gravel roads 349 mi. north from Whitehorse, or by air). Barkerville (see photo) and Ft. Steele are well restored ghosts for the average tourist. Zincton (near Sandon, page 194), Coalmont, Tulameen, and Granite Creek are among British Columbia's truest ghosts for off-the-beaten-track buffs. The Alaskan and Yukon towns are picturesque partial ghosts of the intensive but short-lived Klondike rush.

The Northwest

DE LAMAR, IDAHO (Southwest of Boise; southeast off U.S. 95 from a point about 11 mi. south of where 95 crosses into Oregon; or else east from Jordan Valley, about 10 mi. farther south; either way involves more than 10 mi. of rough, unpaved road; also accessible due west from Silver City—see page 173—on an even rougher road). A true ghost town, for purists. Most impressive structure is the hotel (see photo), with shanty stores, cabins, and mining remnants also dotted along the road. Originally a staging stop between Silver City and Jordan Valley, in the 1890's De Lamar swelled into a "string town" nearly two miles in length as entrepreneur Joseph R. De Lamar worked the canyon's silver mines for a reported yield of $8 million. In a narrow, arid canyon cut by a fast stream.

GRANITE, OREGON (9 mi. south of Baker on State 7, then 20 mi. northwest on State 220 to Sumpter which is also a ghost town. From Sumpter continue northwest on State 220 15 mi. on partly paved road whose condition varies—alternative routes shown on many maps are not recommended). Despite its isolated location, Granite, which was once a pure ghost town, has become increasingly well known. Some of its old houses are now occupied at least part of the year, and a general store is open. Ghost town elements include an old nickelodeon and store (see photo), and other false-fronted structures; a tiny schoolhouse and city hall; and, in a forest of ponderosa pines, a fine old graveyard. Beautifully set in grassy meadows, surrounded by the wild, heavily forested Blue Mountains.

JACKSONVILLE, OREGON (5 mi. west of Medford on State 238). A tourist-conscious non-ghost, analogous to many of California's gold rush towns, with a number of brick buildings dating from the mining camp days of the 1850's and 1860's. The stoutness of Jacksonville's architecture was in part a defense against recurrent fires, floods, and Indian raids. On view are a lovely cemetery, a Protestant church dating from 1851, a well-stocked museum including the restored studio of photographer Peter Britt, and the main street buildings which house a scattering of tourist shops. A gentle landscape, with many varieties of deciduous trees.

RICHMOND, OREGON (Southeast of The Dalles; from about 70 mi. west of John Day on U.S. 26, 19 mi. north on State 207, then 1/3 mi. east on gravel road). A small, very quiet, true ghost. The little town of Richmond was a casualty of the decline in ranching throughout these rolling prairies of northcentral Oregon after the turn of the century. Still remaining are a schoolhouse, quaintly set in the center of a fenced dell; a boarding house-and-community center; and a classic little Methodist church. The grassy, gentle hills are studded with junipers and poplars.

CORNUCOPIA, OREGON (55 mi. east of Baker on State 86, then 11 mi. north on a partly paved road). Once a top-rated ghost, but many structures collapsed under heavy snows in 1969 and 1970. Two or three small commercial buildings remain, plus extensive mining and milling works, cabins, etc. Cornucopia's population swelled to over 700 after the initial boom of 1884-6. Though rich, the quartz gold deposits were capriciously spaced, and the town's fortunes rose and fell erratically. Today, only a few old-timers remain. The heavily forested Wallowa Mountains offer a lush setting.

DOGGEDLY TRUDGING in the footsteps of the old Spanish gold seekers, early American prospectors set out into New Mexico's arid Cerrillos hills. Lying to the south of present-day Santa Fe, the Cerrillos became the first important mining district in the Southwest and is today the site of several ghost towns.

5

THE SOUTHWEST
TOO TOUGH TO DIE
1860...

TOTING WATER AND A SIX-GUN, the man who chose to tramp across the wasted reaches of Arizona and New Mexico, looking for gold, left later generations plenty of colorful lore with which to shape our image of the western hero. For he braved threats more deadly than those faced by prospectors anywhere else in the West: bitterly hostile Indians, extreme scarcity of water, searing heat, stubborn ores, merciless border bandits, and fragile lines of supply. No wonder towns were slow to appear in the Southwest. And no wonder they became famous for their toughness.

Spanish fortune hunters had passed this way before, only to meet eventual failure. Coronado, marching north through the Rio Grande Valley in the early 1540's, never found his fabled cities of gold. Spaniards of the seventeenth century, reputedly forcing Indian slaves to dig for silver in the hills south of present-day Santa Fe, ultimately faced revolt. In 1828 and for a few years after, while still under the Mexican flag, the same hills played host to "America's first gold rush," though this petered out because of political intrigue and the shortage of water. But in the generations following Coronado, peaceful Spanish farmers had settled in New Mexico, and the dustblown residue of their gentle adobe settlements—some think Cabezón flourished as early as 1775—created some of the most unusual ghost towns in the West.

By the time of the major mining rushes farther north, no one doubted that there were valuable ores in the Southwest. The question was how to get them out—how to travel there in the first place, how to extract the "pay" from the recalcitrant gravels and rocks, and how to survive the experience. Not long after the last portions of Arizona and New Mexico were brought under U.S. sovereignty by the Gadsden Purchase of 1853, however, the Americans started arriving. The mining towns they built—and then abandoned—trace their slow, painful subduing of the hostile environment. Today's ghosts thus reflect the evolution of the Southwest from its earliest and wildest days right down to the industrialized present. New Mexico, scene of the earliest activity, boomed and then declined in fairly classic fashion. But Arizona, last of the western mining states to develop, kept right on going, increasing her base-metal yield until her mining industry far outstripped that of her more precocious neighbors.

It's a long drive between southwestern ghost towns—they are not as concentrated as in California's gold rush regions, or Colorado's—and the topography is surprisingly varied. A precariously-perched mountain ghost such as Mogollon, New Mexico, can be snowbound while its southern cousins are still baking in the sun. Such differences make for an interesting range of building styles and materials. They also mean that the prospective ghost-towner will do well to refresh his knowledge of southwestern geography before striking out. Very few of the better haunts require off-the-road travel, but many of them are tough on springs and shock absorbers. And some of those basics which were crucial to yesterday's prospectors are still important: reliable transportation, all-weather clothing, and emergency water. For out-and-out explorers, the New Mexico Bureau of Mines and Mineral Resources publishes a fascinatingly detailed ghost town map which also shows the location of Indian ruins and old military forts.

X True Ghost Town: Majority of buildings disused; few if any residents; no modern facilities.

✸ Partial Ghost Town: Some disused buildings; some residents; limited facilities.

★ Tourist Ghost Town: Old structures refurbished to promote old-time atmosphere; modern facilities.

🛡40 Interstate Highways

🛡80 U.S. Highways

🛡95 State Highways & Secondary Roads

NOTE: Map is as accurate as present information permits. Refer to detailed maps for minor roads, and always inquire locally about road conditions.

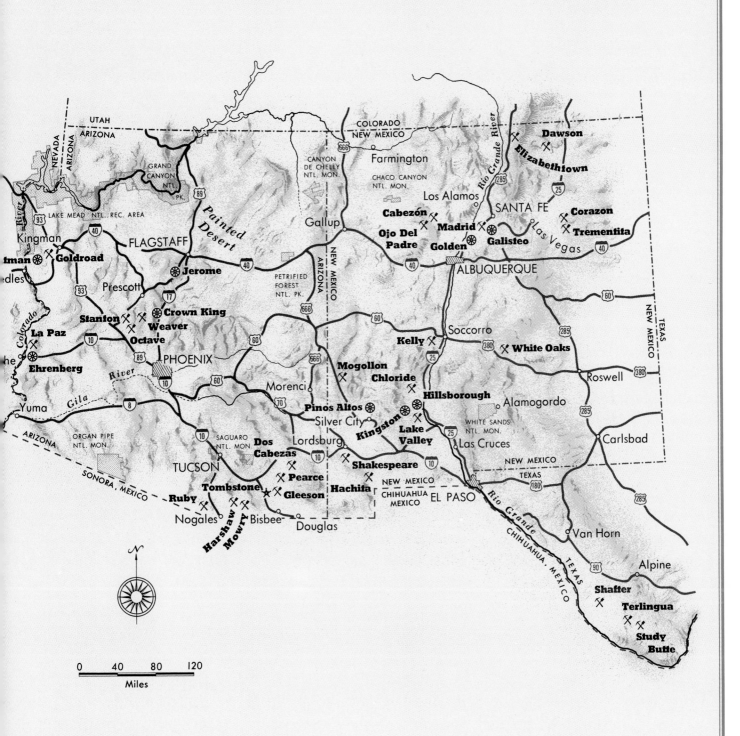

Spanish Ghosts: THE TEXTURES OF CENTURIES

While the missions express the finest of the Spanish
colonial architecture, the down-to-earth lives of
the Spanish-speaking settlers themselves are
reflected in these adobe ghost towns, whose typically
Spanish motifs were modified by the southwestern
environment and by the native pueblo style.

CASA SALAZAR,
at the ghost town of Ojo Del
Padre, New Mexico, has
doors (far left) carved in a
typically Spanish motif. A
painting on animal hide was
found in the little church
at Galisteo, New Mexico,
(left).

EARTHEN textures of a house at
the ghost town of Corazon, New
Mexico, reveal a mixture of
Spanish and native Indian
building methods.

GETTING THE RICHES: THE ARRASTRA

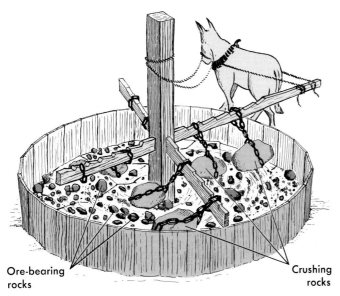

CENTURIES-OLD rock crushing
device, the arrastra, has been
used throughout the world, was
introduced into the American
West by Spanish-speaking miners.
Slow but surprisingly effective, it
depended on abrasive boulders
smashing the ore-bearing rocks to
sand or powder. Many old
arrastras can still be found.

Ore-bearing
rocks

Crushing
rocks

CABEZÓN, NEW MEXICO
FOR TWO HUNDRED YEARS, SE HABLA ESPAÑOL

a GHOST TOWN worth seeing

From Albuquerque go north eighteen miles on Interstate 25, then forty-five miles northwest on State 44 to State 279, a gravel road which exits west and reaches Cabezón after about five miles.

The Navajos called the mountain "The Giant's Head" and used it to define the eastern edge of their nation. By 1767, the Spaniards were coming to ranch and farm under its lofty gaze. They founded a little town and, translating the Navajo term approximately as "Cabezón" ("Big Head"), they gave their settlement this name. Then the Navajos objected to the white man's presence. Over the years, they attacked again and again; but always the Spaniards returned. Not until Kit Carson defeated the Navajos in 1863 could the settlers really settle.

Then they were confronted by water problems. Either the Rio Puerco was a dismal muddy trickle, or it raged down the arroyo, shattering the works of nature and man alike. In time, the Spaniards learned to build dams. But when even these were carried away by flooding in the 1930's and 40's, the people finally gave up. After so long a struggle, Cabezón succumbed.

The silent town faced a new peril: vandals. They smashed through locked doors to steal what they could find; they broke every window pane in town; they even attacked the church and attempted to steal its bell. But "cabezón" also means "stubborn," and again the West's most venerable ghost acquired a Spanish-speaking defender—rancher Stacey Lucero. He owns property in Cabezón, and he is armed. However, if you get on the good side of Stacey, he may prove hospitable. As one visitor found, "Stacey tells you of livelier days in Cabezón: of the spirited cowboy, who when feeling his liquor, would ride his horse right into the bars and dance halls, and who once rode into the schoolhouse and roped the teacher. He speaks of an old man who long ago lived across the river, a solitary man who buried gold under the posts of his corral. The corral is still standing today and perhaps the gold is still under one of those decaying posts."

TOWN'S NAME and much of its character derive from nearby Cabezón Peak, an ancient volcanic plug whose cinder cone fell away. Dominating the landscape for miles around, the mountain inspired legends among many Indian tribes.

Warpath: THE INDIAN THREAT TO THE MINING CAMPS

The hostile Indian relations which had marked the Spanish rule were passed along, and sometimes aggravated, as the Southwest came more and more under Yankee influence. Not all southwestern Indians were dangerous or savage by any means, and not all white men were prejudicial to Indian interests; but there was enough ignorance and hostility on both sides to engender serious strife well into the 1880's. The main tribes threatening both Americans and Mexicans were the Navajos and Apaches, who fought, not as organized defenders of territory in the manner of the Sioux and Plains Indians, but as raiders and plunderers.

The U.S. Army's systematic campaign against the Navajos in 1860 and 1861 was interrupted by the Civil War—with an interesting side effect. To replace the regulars recalled for war duty, units of the "California Volunteers" were garrisoned in Arizona. Once a miner, always a miner: the old Californians couldn't resist sampling the relatively untouched ores in their off-hours. After the war, a number of them stayed on, bringing inspiration and know-how to a fledgling industry.

Meanwhile, Kit Carson was brought in to fight the Navajos. By 1863 he had taken most of them prisoner, and in 1868 the Navajos signed a peace treaty, living quietly on their reservation thereafter. But the Apaches were harder to subdue. Adept at guerilla tactics, and split into many sub-tribes which occasionally fought one another, they could not be dealt with as a whole. They attacked the early mining camps repeatedly and were largely responsible for the wholesale abandonment of the gold community of Pinos Altos in southern New Mexico (after subsequent ups and downs, Pinos Altos is again a virtual ghost). The hard-to-pin-down Apaches could only be fought little by little; and not until the final surrender of Geronimo in 1886 was the Indian threat overcome.

FAMOUS APACHE, Geronimo, took over his Chiricahua tribe in 1881 and terrorized both sides of the U.S.-Mexican border for five years. So wily and unpredictable was he that thousands of troops were needed to subdue his two- or three-dozen braves.

KIT CARSON roamed the West
leading Army units against Indian
tribes. His adobe home at the
semi-ghost town of Rayado, New
Mexico, includes a fortress-like
watchtower.

VICTIM of Zuni tomahawking
lies in a frontier hospital.
Scrawled on the old photo
is the legend: "Head split/
brains out/still alive."

GHOST TOWN of Oatman, Arizona,
was named for Olive Oatman and her family.
Apaches killed the parents, enslaved
Olive and her sister and tattooed them
(note chin). The sister died, but Olive
was ransomed after five years, married a New
Yorker, and lived happily to the age of 68.

NOT ALL RELATIONS with the Indians were
hostile. Many a grizzled Yankee pioneer
lived with an Indian squaw. This couple
was photographed in 1889.

Thirst or Flood? BOTH COULD KILL A SAGEBRUSH TOWN

What traveler can fail to notice the wind-mills dotted all through the southwestern deserts? Spinning gaily—or forever stilled—they speak eloquently of a problem crucial to any settler who wished to till the arid earth or extract its gold. It is hardly surprising that some of the earliest mining towns were in mountainous regions, which were blessed by more rain than the desert floor; yet the lifeline of even a mountain town often consisted of a mule track threading across the wastelands. In Arizona and New Mexico annual rainfall is meager, evaporation rapid, and the water table problematical; when rain does come, it often rages in a torrent, sweeping down the arroyos to wash away livestock, bridges, mining operations—even whole sections of a town.

By painful experience, the early inhabitants learned to live with the situation. The Indians practiced irrigation and developed a special hybrid desert corn. Spanish ranchers chose their sites carefully; and Spanish miners, painstakingly gathering the winter snow, led donkeys loaded with precious kegs of water to the sluice boxes.

The Americans brought along some knowledge acquired in California, learned what they could from the resident Spaniards, and planned grandiose new schemes involving dams, reservoirs, and pipelines. Some succeeded, some didn't. "New Mexico needs less Holy Water and more rain," grumbled one investor. Even Thomas Edison failed: he journeyed thousands of miles to set up a lab near Dolores—now a ghost town in the Cerrillos area—where he spent $2 million in a vain effort to perfect an electrostatic process for extracting placer gold without water.

Success, when it came, would come only gradually. In the meantime, the twin spectres of thirst and flood played an important part in creating the ghost towns of today.

NO CHARGE was made for rainwater rinses as flood after flood struck Bisbee, a copper mining town in southern Arizona. By the early 1970's Bisbee's population had shrunk from 25,000 to 8,000, and as the mines continued to close, there was speculation that Bisbee could become a modern ghost town.

STRUGGLE FOR WATER in an arid land left this battered windmill looming over the ghost town of Lake Valley, New Mexico.

ELIZABETHTOWN, NEW MEXICO
FIGHTING FOR LIFE

a GHOST TOWN worth seeing

From Taos, go thirty-two miles northeast on State 64 to Eagle Nest. Turn left on State 38 and continue five miles to Elizabethtown, which consists of scattered structures a few hundred yards west of the road.

CLASSICALLY ARCHED portals of Elizabethtown's town hall frame the shoulders of Baldy Mountain. This stone edifice is the town's only surviving commercial structure.

For ghost-towners with plenty of imagination, "E-town" offers clues to a rough-and-tumble past. Born in 1867 with the discovery of gold on nearby Baldy Mountain, it was one of the first mining camps in the Southwest to successfully brave the water shortage, Indians, and badmen. Elizabethtown profited from an influx of miners disillusioned with played-out prospects in Colorado, and in 1870 it became the first town to be incorporated into the territory of New Mexico.

E-town's tussle with the water problem reached a peak in 1869, when an ambitious system of flumes and ditches brought water to the placers from the Red River, some forty miles away. Though a remarkable achievement in its time, the waterworks disappointed its inventors by delivering only a small fraction of the volume they had counted on. Scattered remnants of the old flumes can still be found today.

The other peril — violence — came in many forms. While the U.S. Army was helping to subdue the Apaches, the townspeople organized their own militia. A vigilante committee also sprang up, but wild events seemed to snowball. The worst was the case of Charles Kennedy, who for years lured visitors to his dinner table and then killed them with an ax, throwing their bodies into the cellar. Finally the E-towners lynched him, cut off his head, and took it to Cimarron, where it was posted on a stake in front of a saloon as a warning to all and sundry wrongdoers.

After 1875 Elizabethtown died and revived several times before becoming the total ghost it is today. The husk of only one substantial building—the town hall—remains. But you can poke around among the few sagging shacks and widely strewn artifacts; prowl the silent gold gulches with names like Grouse, Pine Tree, Michigan, St. Louis, and Humbug; look over the slopes of Mount Baldy for old mines; and muse over a fabled lode in the very center of the mountain, which was often sought—but never found.

"IT MAKES ONE LONESOME to walk the streets of Elizabethtown,"
wrote an editor as early as 1882: "a sort of graveyard stillness,
deserted buildings . . ." Year by year, the bunch grass has continued
to reclaim those buildings.

Transportation: THE CAMPS' LIFELINE

Travel was a dangerous business in the Southwest. Hostile Indians, border bandits, lack of water, and searing heat discouraged miners and freighters alike, and seriously retarded the growth of towns. But once the railroad arrived, the mining camps grew swiftly.

TRAIN PASSENGERS enjoyed new speed and security.

COLORADO RIVER was an important artery of commerce to such early gold camps as Ehrenberg and La Paz, Arizona, now ghost towns.

FREIGHT trains were crucial in supplying building materials and hauling ores.

LATEST thing in horseless transportation didn't save Courtland, Arizona from becoming a ghost town.

WAGONMASTER and his train pose near Chloride, New Mexico, now a ghost town. Hazards of wagoneering discouraged settlement of the Southwest until late in the nineteenth century.

a GHOST TOWN worth seeing

From Santa Fe, go southwest ten miles on Interstate 25, then turn south on State 10 and continue seventeen miles south to Madrid, which straddles the highway. Historic Cerrillos is on the way, and the partial ghosts of Galisteo and Golden are also nearby.

PROUD SURVIVOR of years of abandonment, this picturesque rooming house was the first home in America for many of the European immigrants who were brought over to work in Madrid's coal mines.

One of America's classically pure ghost towns, Madrid has history all its own. Although situated in the Ortiz Mountains, among many remnants of the early gold-digging days, Madrid neither came early nor dug gold.

Instead, blessed with an extremely rare combination of both hard and soft coal deposits, Madrid fed the railroads and was fed by them. The *Atchison, Topeka and Santa Fe* ran the town in the late 1880's and early 90's. From then on there was a succession of operators and owners. The biggest year was 1928, when the mines shipped over 180,000 tons of anthracite and bituminous. Then came the depression, plus increasing competition from other fuel sources. During World War II, Madrid perked up again, as a laboratory called Los Alamos began buying huge amounts of coal for purposes the townspeople could only guess at. But when the war ended, the atomic station changed over to natural gas. And when the railroads switched from coal to diesel. Madrid succumbed.

Ghost town buffs will recognize all the features of a typical company town: long rows of identical frame dwellings, an orderly layout so different from the helter-skelter sprawl of other mining camps, and the obvious centralization of enterprise. The present owners charge a small fee to let you meander at will among an outstanding collection of artifacts, both outdoors and in. The great mine structures by the mountain are off-limits, and it takes luck and persistence to get directions to the cemetery. But Madrid is readily accessible and well worth a visit.

UNIFORMITY OF LIFE in a company town is emphasized by these long rows of tract houses still standing. They rented for $2 per room per month, including coal, with an extra charge of 50¢ for electric lights.

ELABORATE celebrations were a source of special pride in Madrid. Her Christmas lighting gained national fame, and the Fourth of July parade (left) stretched the length of the main street. Yet even on a holiday the mill belched smoke. And was the upside-down flag the work of a wag or someone in international distress?

RUSTING steam engine watches over Madrid. The Atchison, Topeka, and Santa Fe operated this coal town for some years, and the West's burgeoning railways were always prime customers. But when they changed over to diesel fuel, Madrid died.

A Vanished Grit: MINING CAMPS OF THE BLACK RANGE

New Mexico's first important group of American mining camps sprang up in the hills around Pinos Altos, in the southwestern part of the State. But the Apaches were unkind, and time has been even more unkind, to these flinty but long-defunct settlements.

LIKE ACTORS pausing for a publicity shot, citizens of Kingston, New Mexico, pose in front of their newly built homes. Born in 1880, Kingston soon had twenty-seven silver mines and a population of more than seven thousand. But the crashing silver market of 1893 killed the town. All that has survived is one bank—with a jail conveniently attached.

BULLDOGGING a steer revealed the cowboy heritage of Chloride, New Mexico, now a ghost town. Note that the Americans have grafted a wooden false front onto an existing adobe building.

GAILY PARADING down the main street of Mogollon, New Mexico, Mexican miners celebrate the traditional holiday of "Cinco de Mayo" (Fifth of May).

Swinging the Doors: FUN WAS WHERE YOU FOUND IT

In the isolated towns of the Southwest, there was little in the way of ready-made entertainment. Thrown on their own resources, the citizens amused themselves with sports and celebrations that were usually as vigorous as they were simple.

UNIVERSAL SPORT throughout the early West was prizefighting, and sometimes the match took place in a saloon. Here in Mogollon, the referee distinguished himself from the rabble with a Victorian mustachio and lack of hat.

MOGOLLON, NEW MEXICO
BAD PROBLEMS, GOOD ORE

a GHOST TOWN worth seeing

From Lordsburg, take U.S. 70 and State 90 northeast to Silver City. Take U.S. 180 sixty-four miles northwest to Glenwood; continue another five miles to State 78, turn right, go ten miles to Mogollon. Maps show State 78 crossing the mountains from the east, but this route should never be tried without local advice.

SHARP TURNS—STEEP GRADE—TRAILERS OVER 20 FT. UNSAFE bellows the big sign as you start up the western slope of the Mogollon (pronounced "mo-gee-yon") Range in Gila National Forest. If you're a normally cautious driver, don't be dissuaded. And yet the unfenced hairpin turns, which overlook vertical precipices, may make you wonder what life was like for the early freighters. Inching along a narrow shelf hacked out of the cliffs by convict labor in 1897, the twenty-mule teamsters charged $50 a ton to haul out raw ore assaying at perhaps $200 a ton. Once down on the flatlands, they encountered more problems: there, the clay mud was sometimes so deep that it took whole days to move a few hundred yards. Mogollon profited greatly when better ways were found for concentrating and extracting low-grade silver and gold at the source.

The Indian problem was also severe. Having chosen these mountains as their final stronghold, the Apaches killed many miners. Yet, blessed with some of the State's richest precious metal deposits, Mogollon struggled through, and by 1914 its payrolls neared $1 million a year. Business was good until 1926; after that came the familiar story of declining ups and downs until after World War II, when everything closed for good.

Today there are many old mine structures scattered over the steep hillsides; a section of broken-out houses above the town; and among the abandoned buildings of the town proper, a lunch counter and post office, a quaint, kerosene-lighted museum, and a couple of artists-in-residence. If you haven't come to plunder, the slow-going locals are friendly and knowledgeable about Mogollon's colorful past—just so long as you pronounce it right.

PATCHWORK of sheet metal serves as the facade of a tiny, unnamed structure dozing between J. P. Holland's General Store and the tumbledown Mogollon Theater.

ABANDONED house is one of the many empty buildings clustered around the Little Fanny mill, above Mogollon.

HUGE MILL COMPLEX
of the Little Fanny Mine commands a view
of the precipitous approach to Mogollon
from the Frisco Valley, beyond. The chalky
white tailings resulted from treating gold
ore with cyanide.

CORE SAMPLES (far left) are among the scattered debris of the Little Fanny Mine. Cyanide boxes from Canada were used to build a shed (left). Use of the chemical, one of the few that dissolves gold, marked advance in refining technology.

Good Guys, Bad Guys, AND A BAD GAL

Every corner of the Old West spawned its share of highwaymen, cardsharks, claimjumpers, good marshals, bad marshals, and vigilantes. But the Southwest drew the roughest customers of all. The renegades of the Dodge Cities and Virginia Cities came pouring into this final frontier as if bent on one last shootout.

WYATT EARP: card-sharp, gunman, deputy marshal, Tombstone, Arizona.

BILLY THE KID: alias William Bonney. Hired gun to both sides in cattle wars. Killed 15 by age 17. Eluded man-hunts, broke out of jail, was shot dead at age 21.

PEARL HART: disguised as a man, allegedly committed the West's last stagecoach robbery in 1899.

VIRGIL EARP: marshal,
Tombstone, Arizona; crippled
by buckshot wounds.

DOC HOLLIDAY: dentist,
gambler, coldest blooded
killer of Earp faction.

BLACK JACK KETCHUM:
train robber, liked to beat own
head with six-shooter.

JEFF MILTON: Texas Ranger,
Wells Fargo Messenger,
U.S. Customs and Border Agent.

JOE PHY: deputy sheriff,
killed in gunfight, Tunnel
Saloon, Florence, Arizona.

ROBERT PAUL: Wells Fargo
Special Agent, U.S. Marshal,
Arizona Territory.

TOMBSTONE, ARIZONA
TOUGHEST OF THE TOUGH

a GHOST TOWN worth seeing

From Tucson, go forty-four miles southeast on Interstate 10 to Benson, then twenty-six miles southeast on U.S. 80 to Tombstone. Mining buffs will also want to see the spectacular open-pit copper mine at Bisbee, twenty-six miles south.

Ghost town purists may turn up their noses at Tombstone: it's an out-and-out commercialized restoration like those at Columbia, California, Virginia City, Nevada, and Central City, Colorado. Yet a fabled history does walk these streets, and it's worth considering, as you perch in the gloom of the old Bird Cage Theatre or swagger in the hot glare of the O.K. Corral, what Tombstone might have been like, had it been allowed to crumble into the dust.

"Some day you'll find your tombstone," a soldier at Fort Huachuca, Arizona Territory, told the lone prospector in 1877. But Ed Schieffelin would not be dissuaded. Born—perhaps prophetically—in 1848, he had grown up in California, and searched for gold and silver in Nevada, Utah, Oregon, and Idaho before deciding to try his luck in this new, raw frontier. The soldiers were combing the countryside for Geronimo's Apaches, and Schieffelin rode with them until he learned the lay of the land.

Then he struck out alone, heading east into the San Pedro Valley. Camping on the highest hill for security, he suddenly spotted an outcropping of silver ore. Though excited, Schieffelin realized he would need money to work the claim. He went to his brother, who was mining farther north, for help. An assayer valued the ore at $2,000 a ton and promptly staked the brothers. The three returned to the strike—and found a lode assaying at $15,000 to the ton. Word got out; the rush was on. With typical frontier humor, Schieffelin had named his first claim the Tombstone, and the camp soon acquired the same name. As the mines poured out their millions, it swelled to a city of 15,000.

Tombstone boasted five newspapers, including one of the most famous in the West, the *Epitaph*, which is still going. The saloons were fancy, the strumpets brazen, the restaurants elegant, the characters fabulous, and the theaters among the best in the West. Even when the mines declined, Tombstone never entirely died. The county seat until 1929, it was by then already becoming a tourist center. Since 1964, some $3 million has been spent on its careful restoration. If you're a modern assayer of Western lore, one of your best investments may be the fourth-part-of-a-dollar asked for the "Tombstone Map and Guide," describing 45 of the town's unique attractions.

COVERED BOARDWALKS of downtown Tombstone lead visitors to the pure and puerile of Western Americana. Besides the commercial shops, there are well-restored buildings and fine collections.

MOST FAMOUS SHOOTOUT in the history of the West erupted at the
O.K. Corral as the climax to a bitter feud between Marshal Wyatt
Earp and the Clanton outlaws. Tombstone still celebrates such
wild doings in its annual "Helldorado Days" and other events. This
photograph was taken in 1930.

...TOMBSTONE, ARIZONA...

SO INTENT on fortune's turn were these chips-off-the-old-block that they seemed not to notice the cameraman who caught them in action in a Tombstone saloon.

TOMBSTONE, ARIZONA, 1882

MANY of the buildings shown on this map of old Tombstone can still be seen. The outstanding ones are shown in color.

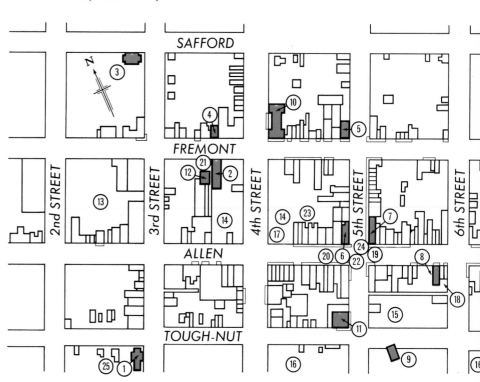

1. Cochise County Courthouse
2. Tombstone City Hall
3. Episcopal Church
4. Tombstone Epitaph Office
5. San Jose House (lodging)
6. Crystal Palace Saloon
7. Oriental Saloon
8. Bird Cage Theatre
9. Firehouse
10. Schieffelin Hall
11. Russ House (lodging)
12. OK Corral
13. Mountain Maid Mine
14. Ruins
15. Combination Mine
16. Miners' Cabins
17. Frank Leslie shot Mike Eilleen, 1880
18. Curly Bill shot Marshal Fred White, 1881
19. Luke Short shot Charlie Storms, 1881
20. Wyatt Earp held off a lynch mob of 500, 1881
21. OK Corral Fight: Billy Clanton, Frank and
    Tom McLowery shot by the Earps, 1881
22. Virgil Earp ambushed and wounded, 1881
23. Morgan Earp assassinated, 1882
24. Frank Leslie shot Billy Claiborne, 1882
25. Howard, Kelley, Sample, Dowd, and Delaney
    hanged for Bisbee Massacre, 1884

The New Miner: A CHANGING COMMUNITY HAD CHANGED HIS LIFE

In the Southwest, industrial mining often required the building of company towns. Now, instead of living on a grubstake, the miners carried lunch-buckets. Instead of scanning the hills, they crawled under the earth. And the individualism of the old prospectors gave way to collective bargaining.

SOME LONERS held out against the industrial age, and still do. This independent miner is working a small claim at the ghost town of Kingston, New Mexico.

FLANNEL shirts were donned by miners
fearful of catching cold as they emerged
dripping wet from the hot, stifling tunnels. The
men in sweaters are foremen.

NOTICE

TO ALL MEMBERS
OF
UNITED MINE WORKERS OF AMERICA

This mine is in Government possession and
will remain open. Your contract with the
Government remains effective, as it very
plainly says, for "the period of Government
possession." The Government and all the
people of the country expect the miners
to honor their contract and to mine the
coal which the nation needs.

Secretary of the Interior.

ELABORATE RULES governed the
movements of the new miners,
and in time of national emergency,
the government had to override
the usual process of collective
bargaining.

JEROME, ARIZONA
THE BIG ONE

a GHOST TOWN worth seeing

From Phoenix, take Interstate 17 seventy-four miles north to Camp Verde. Then take State 279 sixteen miles northwest to intersection with U.S. 89 Alternate; turn left, go ten miles farther northwest to town of Jerome.

BELIEVE IT OR NOT,
a candlelit gourmet restaurant, the House of Joy, stands right across the street from this scene. Jerome's strangely juxtaposed elements vary from pure-ghost, to hip-artist, to garden-variety tourist.

Whether approaching from the Verde Valley below, or down the mountains from Prescott, you can't help but realize a key fact about Jerome long before you get there: it is perched precariously on a steep hillside. Serpentine switchbacks carry you past the mouldering hulks of big old wooden houses and concrete buildings, most of them clearly of twentieth-century vintage. The highest are 1,500 feet above the lowest—at best an approximate figure, since Jerome's structures, including the old concrete jail, have a bothersome habit of slithering down the 30° incline.

As you explore this sober, broad-shouldered ghost, you begin to see that it lived, not among the zany speculations of get-rich-quick prospectors, but under the careful control of big corporate enterprise. Consider, for instance, that the ground you stand on is undercut by some 80 miles of tunnels. Consider that Jerome pulled eight hundred million dollars out of that ground between 1885 and 1953—mostly in copper ores, but also in silver and gold. And consider that the barren, surrounding slopes, including blackened Cleopatra Hill directly above the town, were forested in oak and pine until the deadly smelter fumes and lumber saws did their work.

The setting is nevertheless spectacular, and Jerome has begun to capitalize on its picturesqueness by attracting artists, weekenders, and others. There are two good museums, a Methodist church sheathed with powder boxes, a huge old hospital, and many other attractions. Happily, there's a minimum of hokum, and Jerome's description of itself as "the largest ghost city in America" may still be valid.

SPECTACULAR VIEW across the Verde Valley to the red cliffs of Oak Creek Canyon was afforded guests of the Little Daisy Hotel, which now rests in lonely isolation near the abandoned mine for which it was named.

FAR CRY from the helter-skelter mining camps of frontier days, these sober, orderly houses point up Jerome's role as a big-production mining town.

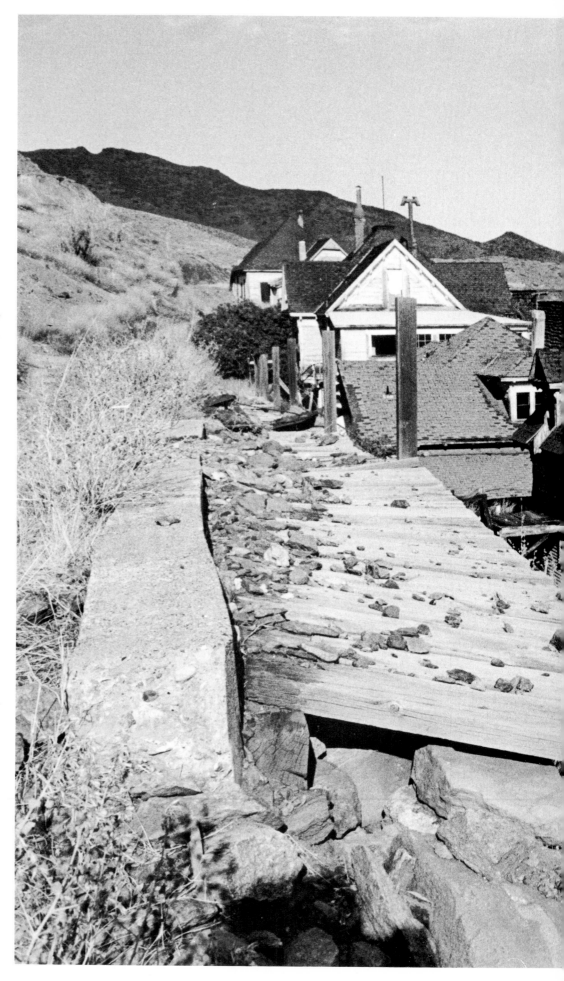

PERCHED precariously on the thirty-degree slant of Cleopatra Hill, Jerome's many-styled buildings recall the varied phases of the copper camp's long, colorful history.

SAGGING storefronts of downtown Jerome have a twentieth-century ghost town quality all their own.

FAMOUS FATHERS and sons of Jerome include United States Senator William A. Clark (left) and U.S. Ambassador to Great Britain, Lewis W. Douglas (above). Clark bought the faltering United Verde Company in 1885 and pumped a million dollars into an expansion program that made Jerome boom. Then ''Rawhide Jimmy'' Douglas bought the Little Daisy claim and grossed $125 million on it. Lewis, his son, though groomed to become a Jerome capitalist, chose a life of international politics, finance, and education, and gave his Jerome house to the State of Arizona as a museum.

RANCHOS DE TAOS, NEW MEXICO

ARROYO HONDO, NEW MEXICO

DAWSON, NEW MEXICO

MADRID, NEW MEXICO

ELIZABETHTOWN, NEW MEXICO

CERRILLOS, NEW MEXICO

Ghost Markers: THE RICH JOTTINGS OF BOOT HILL AND CAMPOSANTO

From the period of Spanish colonial settlement, through the meteoric rise and fall of the first American mining camps, and on into the era of sober industrial growth, the long history of Southwestern America is retold in its grave markers.

JEROME, ARIZONA

QUESTA, NEW MEXICO

SETTLERS of Spanish origin carved beautiful wooden gravemarkers. Early Yankee boot hills also showed some interesting carving (Elizabethtown, Cerrillos). Miners from Europe preferred classical gravestones (Madrid, Jerome). Metal was used in the mass burial of miners killed in an explosion (Dawson) and in some homemade markers (Golden).

GOLDEN, NEW MEXICO

GOLDEN AND CERRILLOS, NEW MEXICO (South of Santa Fe, south off U.S. 85 on State 10). State 10 makes an easy and logical tourist route through the Southwest's oldest mining region—the Ortiz, San Pedro, and Cerrillos mountains. It includes Madrid (see pp. 226-9) as well as Golden and Cerrillos. Also worth a visit are nearby Galisteo and a number of old mines east of Golden. Chief attractions at Golden are the beautiful church and churchyard (see photo). Although Cerrillos' famous cemeteries have been vandalized, the town proper has become a mini-center for summer tourists, featuring such authentic Victorian buildings as the Tiffany Saloon, the old Palace Hotel, and a melodrama theater. Arid, gently rolling hills.

WHITE OAKS, NEW MEXICO (East of Socorro, north of Carrizozo on State 349). Billy the Kid hung out here. Only two buildings of interest remain, but both are good—the grandiosely façaded old store and bank; and, on a little rise, "Hoyle's Folly," a spare-no-expense Victorian mansion built for a bride who never appeared. After thriving on gold in the 1880's, White Oaks killed itself by overpricing its rail right-of-way and thus losing the railroad. Good unpaved road through barren desert hill country.

TREMENTINA AND CORAZON, NEW MEXICO (East of Las Vegas, 4 mi. northeast off State 104 between Trujillo and Variadero on unpaved State 65). Very lonely, sparsely settled cattle country. Corazon is off the road altogether, so be sure to have all the topographical maps and local advice you can get before attempting to find it. Little is known of the history of these Spanish-speaking settlements, but the architecture, like the red-earth-and-mesa landscape, is pure Southwest.

SHAKESPEARE, NEW MEXICO (West of Las Cruces, 5 mi. southwest of Lordsburg). A pure, adobe-walled, classically Southwestern ghost town with a wild history of bandits, diamond hoaxes, silver mines, and Indian-chasing soldiers. Mrs. Rita Hill, who owns the whole battered town, gives conducted tours crammed with facts and local lore. Her own home, an ancient edifice full of historic artifacts, is included. Somewhat incongruously, her daughter, Janaloo, operates a modern dancing school for Lordsburgians in another building. Bleak, windblown desert setting, easily accessible. Real buffs may also visit Hachita, some 40 miles southeast.

The Southwest

DOS CABEZAS, ARIZONA (East of Tucson, southeast of U.S. 10 on State 186). Authentic ghost town of plaster-faced adobe ruins, wooden houses, and a dilapidated old stage stop. Braving severe Apache attacks, epidemics, and other hazards, Dos Cabezas subsisted on the relatively modest proceeds of some nearby gold and silver mines from 1878 until after the turn of the century. Desert hills and flatlands.

RUBY, ARIZONA (South of Tucson, west off U.S. 89 at Arivaca Jct., 12 mi. south of Arivaca). One of the Southwest's most extensive pure ghosts. Privately owned, and guarded by caretakers, Ruby may be visited only with permission. Seek advice from voluble Harvey Riggs of Arivaca, who publishes an eccentric newsletter about his corner of the world, *Arivaca Briefs*. The unpaved, direct road from Ruby to U.S. 89 is spectacular but rough. Harshaw and Mowry, east of State 82 near Nogales, are smaller but more readily visitable ghost towns.

GLEESON, COURTLAND, AND PEARCE, ARIZONA (Southeast of Tucson, east and north of Tombstone on unpaved road connecting with U.S. 666). A trio of minor ghosts adding up to an off-beat loop which purists may prefer to bustling Tombstone. Masonry school building (see photo) is Gleeson's chief remnant; Courtland consists of only two small, adjoining, brick-façaded commercial buildings; Pearce includes among its adobe and other ruins a country store and museum. Get precise directions locally, as the roads are subject to change and there are unmarked forks. Desert hills and flatlands.

TERLINGUA AND STUDY BUTTE, TEXAS (Southeast of El Paso, south off U.S. 90 at Alpine on State 118, then State 170, just north of the Rio Grande). Adobe and rock houses, old mine buildings, an officials' residence, and mining artifacts. Beware of open mineshafts. These frontier mercury-mining camps grew explosively after 1890, were killed after World War II by rising costs and stiffening foreign competition. Wild, desolate desert country, often the hottest part of the U.S. in summer. Shafter, on U.S. 67 to the northwest, is another ghost worth visiting.

OATMAN AND GOLDROAD, ARIZONA (32 mi. southwest of Kingman, off U.S. 66). Refurbished for tourists, Oatman boasts a hotel-cum-antique store, old firehouse, etc. The jagged surrounding hills, dotted with old mines, are of interest to rockhounds. Named for kidnapped Olive Oatman (see p. 215), the gold camp boomed between 1903 and the 1930's. Nearby Goldroad, which flourished during the same period, is now a rubbled ruin. Good paved road through arid, treeless hills.

SELECTED READINGS

BOOKS OF GENERAL INTEREST

Eberhart, Perry. *Guide to the Colorado Ghost Towns and Mining Camps*. Chicago, Sage Books, 1959. $8.50.

Florin, Lambert. *Ghost Town Album*. Seattle, Superior Publishing Company, 1962. $12.50.

_____. *Ghost Town Trails*. Seattle, Superior Publishing Company, 1963. $12.50.

_____. *Ghost Town Shadows*. Seattle, Superior Publishing Company, 1964.

_____. *Ghost Town Treasures*. Seattle, Superior Publishing Company, 1965. $12.95.

_____. *Western Ghost Towns*. Seattle, Superior Publishing Company, 1967. $12.50.

_____. *Ghost Town El Dorado*. Seattle, Superior Publishing Company, 1968. $12.95.

_____. *A Guide to Western Ghost Towns*. Seattle, Superior Publishing Company, 1967. $3.95.

Jenkinson, Michael and Kernberger, Karl. *Ghost Towns of New Mexico*. The University of New Mexico Press, 1967. $7.50.

Looney, Ralph. *Haunted Highways—The Ghost Towns of New Mexico*. New York, Hastings House, Publishers, 1968. $12.95.

Murbarger, Nell. *Ghosts of the Adobe Walls*. Los Angeles, Westernlore Press, 1964. $7.50.

_____. *Ghosts of the Glory Trail*. Los Angeles, Westernlore Press, 1956.

Nadeau, Remi. *Ghost Towns and Mining Camps of California*. Los Angeles, The Ward Ritchie Press, 1965. $5.95.

Paher, Stanley W. *Nevada Ghost Towns & Mining Camps*. Berkeley, Howell-North Books, 1970. $15.00.

Rensch, H. E. and E. G.; and Hoover, Mildred. *Historic Spots in California*. Stanford, Stanford University Press, 1966. $10.00.

Sherman, James E. and Barbara H. *Ghost Towns of Arizona*. University of Oklahoma Press, 1969. Paperback $3.95.

Silverberg, Robert. *Ghost Towns of the American West*. New York, Thomas Y. Crowell Company, 1968. $4.50.

Sunset Books. *Gold Rush Country*. Menlo Park, Lane Magazine & Book Company, 1963. $1.95.

Wolle, Muriel Sibell. *Montana Pay Dirt*. Denver, Swallow/Sage Books, 1963. $12.50.

_____. *Stampede to Timberline*. Chicago, Sage Books, 1949. $9.50.

GENERAL HISTORICAL WORKS

Beebe, Lucius and Clegg, Charles. *The American West*. New York, E. P. Dutton & Company, 1955. $14.95.

Greever, William S. *The Bonanza West*. Norman, University of Oklahoma Press, 1963. $7.50.

Horan, James D. *The Great American West*. New York, Crown Publishers, Inc., 1959. $10.00.

Josephy, Alvin M. Jr. (ed.). *The American Heritage History of the Great West*. New York, Simon & Schuster, Inc., 1965. $16.50.

Monaghan, Jay (ed.). *The Book of the American West*. New York, Julian Messner Inc., 1963. $22.50.

Paul, Rodman W. *Mining Frontiers of the Far West 1848-1880*. Holt, Rinehart and Winston, 1963. $8.75; paperback $3.25.

Smith, Charles W. *Pacific Northwest Americana*. Portland, Binfords & Mort, Publishers, 1950. $10.00.

Stone, Irving. *Men to Match my Mountains*. New York, Doubleday & Company, Inc., 1956. $6.95.

SPECIALIZED SUBJECTS

Brown, Robert L. *Ghost Towns of the Colorado Rockies*. Idaho, The Caxton Printers, Ltd., 1969. $6.25.

_____. *Jeep Trails to Colorado Ghost Towns*. Idaho, The Caxton Printers, Ltd., 1968. $5.50.

Cain, Ella M. *The Story of Bodie*. San Francisco, Fearon Publishers, 1956.

Chalfant, W. A. *Gold, Guns & Ghost Towns*. Stanford, California, Stanford University Press, 1947. $3.95.

Davis, Jean. *Shallow Diggin's*. Idaho, The Caxton Printers, Ltd., 1966. $6.50.

Fisher, Vardis and Holmes, Opal Laurel. *Gold Rushes and Mining Camps of the Early American West*. Idaho, The Caxton Printers, Ltd., 1968. $15.00.

Florin, Lambert. *Boot Hill*. Seattle, Superior Publishing Company, 1966. $12.95.

_____. *Historic Western Churches*. Seattle, Superior Publishing Company, 1969. $12.95.

_____. *Tales the Western Tombstones Tell*. Seattle, Superior Publishing Company, 1967. $12.95.

Historic Georgetown, Centennial Gazette 1868-1968. Denver, A. B. Hirschfeld Press, 1968.

Leadabrand, Russ. *Exploring California Byways*. Los Angeles, The Ward Ritchie Press, 1969. $1.95.

_____. *A Guidebook to the Mojave Desert of California*. Los Angeles, The Ward Ritchie Press, 1966. $1.95.

Martin, Douglas D. *Tombstone's Epitaph*. Alburquerque, The University of New Mexico Press, 1951. $5.95.

Morley, Jim and Foley, Doris. *Gold Cities: Grass Valley and Nevada City*. Berkeley, Howell-North Books, 1965. $2.50.

Pence, Mary Lou and Homsher, Lola M. *The Ghost Towns of Wyoming*. New York, Hastings House, Publishers, 1956. $7.50.

Price, Raye Carleson. *Diggins and Doings in Park City*. Salt Lake City, University of Utah Press, 1968. $3.95.

Ramsey, Bruce. *Ghost Towns of British Columbia*. Canada, Mitchell Press, Ltd., 1963.

Webb, Todd. *Gold Strikes and Ghost Towns*. Garden City, N.Y., Doubleday & Company, Inc., 1961. $4.95.

Wolle, Muriel Sibell. *The Bonanza Trail*. Bloomington, Indiana University Press, 1955. $8.50.

Young, Herbert V. *Ghosts of Cleopatra Hill*. Jerome, Arizona, Jerome Historical Society, 1964. $2.25.

SPECIALIZED HISTORICAL WORKS

Allen, James B. *The Company Town in the American West*. Oklahoma, University of Oklahoma Press, 1967. $6.95.

Andrews, Ralph W. *Picture Gallery Pioneers*. New York, Bonanza Books, 1964.

_____. *Photographers of the Frontier West*. Seattle, Superior Publishing Company, 1965. $12.95.

Blumenstein, Lynn. *Bottle Rush U.S.A.* Salem, Oregon, Old Time Bottle Publishing Company, 1966. $4.25.

_____. *Old Time Bottles*. Salem, Oregon, Old Time Bottle Publishing Company, 1966. $2.50.

_____. *Redigging the West*. Salem, Oregon, Old Time Bottle Publishing Company, 1966. $4.25.

Bowlin, Opal M. *Antique Sad Irons*. copyrighted 1965 by Opal M. Bowlin, Yucca Valley, California. $2.00.

Bressie, Wes and Ruby. *Ghost Town Bottle Price Guide*. Yreka, California, News-Journal Print Shop, 1966. $3.00.

Cain, Ella M. *The Story of Early Mono County*. San Franicsco, Fearon Publishers, Inc., 1961. $3.75.

Elliott, Russel R. *Nevada's Twentieth-Century Mining Boom*. Nevada, University of Nevada Press, 1966. $5.95.

Ferraro, Pat and Bob. *A Bottle Collector's Book*. Sparks, Nevada, Western Printing & Publishing Company, 1966. $5.25.

Horan, James D. and Sann, Paul. *Pictorial History of the Wild West*. New York, Crown Publishers, Inc., 1954. $7.50.

Karolevitz, Robert F. *Doctors of the Old West*. Seattle, Superior Publishing Company, 1967. $12.95.

_____. *Newspapering in the Old West*. Seattle, Superior Publishing Company, 1965. $12.95.

Kemble, Edward C. *A History of California Newspapers 1846-1858*. Los Altos, California, The Talisman Press, 1962. $10.00.

Kendrick, Grace. *The Antique Bottle Collector*. Ann Arbor, Michigan, Edwards Brothers, Inc., 1966. $2.50.

Ladd, Richard S. *A Descriptive List of Treasure Maps and Charts*. Washington, D.C., U.S. Government Printing Office, 1964. 30¢.

_____. *Maps Showing Explorers' Routes, Trails & Early Roads in the United States*. Washington, U.S. Government Printing Office, 1962. $1.25.

Mazzulla, Fred M. and Jo. *The First 100 Years*. Detroit, Detroit Publishing Company. $2.00.

Paul, Rodman W. *California Gold: The Beginning of Mining in the Far West*. Lincoln, University of Nebraska Press, 1947. $1.60.

Skibby, Terry. *Antique Bottles*. Ashland, Oregon, Old Bottle Collecting Publications, 1969. $3.00.

Sloane, Howard N. and Lucille N. *A Pictorial History of American Mining*. New York, Crown Publishers, Inc., 1970. $12.50.

Smith, Duane A. *Rocky Mountain Mining Camps*. Bloomington, Indiana University Press, 1967. $6.95.

Smith, Grant H. *The History of the Comstock Lode. 1850-1920*. Reno, Nevada Bureau of Mines, 1943.

Tilden, Freeman. *Following the Frontier with F. Jay Haynes*. New York, Alfred A. Knopf, 1964. $15.00.

Wagner, Jack R. *Gold Mines of California*. Berkeley, Howell-North Books, 1970. $10.00.

Waters, Frank. *The Earp Brothers of Tombstone*. New York, Bramhall House, 1960.

Wynn, Marcia Rittenhouse. *Desert Bonanza-Early Randsburg, Mojave Desert Mining Camp*. Glendale, Ca., The Arthur H. Clark Company, 1963. $8.50.

ACTUAL ACCOUNTS FROM THE TIMES

Billeb, Emil W. *Mining Camp Days*. Berkeley, Howell-North Books, 1968. $5.00.

Browne, J. Ross. *A Peep at Washoe and Washoe Revisited*. Balboa Island, Ca., Paisano Press, 1959. $6.00.

Buffum, E. Gould. *Six Months in the Gold Mines*. Los Angeles, Ward Ritchie Press, 1958. $5.00.

Clappe, Louise. *The Shirley Letters From the California Mines 1851-1852*. New York, Alfred A. Knopf, 1961. $5.95.

DeQuille, Dan. *The Big Bonanza*. New York, Apollo, 1969. Paperback $3.45.

Gower, Harry P. *50 Years in Death Valley—Memorirs of a Borax Man*. San Bernardino, Inland Printing & Engraving Company, 1969.

INDEX

This book was lithographed and bound by Kingsport Press Inc., Kingsport, Tennessee, from film prepared by Graphic Arts Center, Portland, Oregon. Body type is Futura, composed by Holmes Typography, Inc., San Jose, California. Heads are Comstock and Avant Garde, set by Timely Typography, San Francisco, California. Paper for the body is Lane Enamel made by Northwest Paper Co., Cloquet, Minnesota.